New Ways in Using Authentic Materials in the Classroom

Ruth E. Larimer and Leigh Schleicher, Editors,
with Maria H. DaCosta

New Ways in TESOL Series II
Innovative Classroom Techniques
Jack C. Richards, Series Editor

TESOL

Founded 1966

Teachers of English to Speakers of Other Languages, Inc.

Typeset in Garamond Book and Tiffany Demi
by Capitol Communication Systems, Inc., Crofton, Maryland USA
and printed by
Pantagraph Printing, Bloomington, Illinois USA

Teachers of English to Speakers of Other Languages, Inc. (TESOL)
700 South Washington Street, Suite 200
Alexandria, VA 22314 USA
Tel 703-836-0774 • Fax 703-836-7864 • e-mail: tesol@tesol.edu • http://www.tesol.edu/

Director of Communications and Marketing: Helen Kornblum
Managing Editor: Marilyn Kupetz
Cover Design: Ann Kammerer

ISBN 0-939791-80-3
Library of Congress Catalogue No. 98-061418

Contents

Acknowledgments

First and foremost, we would like to thank all of the educators from around the globe who contributed their ideas to this volume. Dedication to sharing information with others is a strength of the profession and a tribute to individuals in it.

Maria DaCosta deserves special recognition. She came along just in time and provided just the right amount of professionalism, organizational ability, and good nature to bring this project to a successful finish.

Thank you also to Jennifer Allen, whose work in the early stages contributed greatly to this project.

Finally, thank you to our colleagues at the Monterey Institute of International Studies. We especially appreciate the help of the following individuals: Beverly Sellmeyer, Peter A. Rogan, Tina Barth-Townend, Sharon Gordon, Kelly Yamamoto, Cristyn Elder, Julie Vorholt, and Paul Firth.

Introduction

Although *authentic materials* has become a catch phrase nearly as ubiquitous as *communicative language teaching,* relatively few of those authentic materials have found their way into language classrooms. This may sometimes be because there are few materials available (as in an EFL setting); it may be because the teacher has no time to develop appropriate pedagogical tasks to accompany such texts; or it may even be that the very definition and usefulness of such materials is unclear. In this book, we hope to demonstrate, by examples, how a whole array of authentic materials can be adapted into interesting and innovative lessons for language learners.

Authentic materials, in the context of the language classroom, include oral and written texts that occur naturally in the target language environment and that have not been created or edited expressly for language learners. There are many advantages to using authentic texts in the classroom. Swaffar (1985) discusses several of these:

1. learning is enhanced by the use of texts of particular interest to a class
2. there will be an increase in variety and spontaneity in classes that introduce authentic materials
3. exposure to a variety of vocabulary and structures will occur
4. students will capitalize on their prior cultural and schematic knowledge to contrast target situations and genres with those of their own culture (p. 18)

Valdman (1992), contrasting instruction based on authentic materials with structure-based proficiency-oriented instruction, asserts that "communicative ability both in the productive and receptive modes, can be attained only if learners are exposed to a variety of authentic oral and written texts illustrating a broad range of genres and pragmatic situations" (p. 88). Cathcart (1989), in a study of medical discourse, and Biber, Conrad, and

Reppen (1994), in an argument for large corpus analysis of authentic texts, point out that *non*authentic text materials often give false impressions of the common usage of given works or phrases. When authentic materials are examined, very different priorities for instruction may emerge.

We would argue that authentic materials have a place in every classroom, from Day 1, and that the simplification that makes these materials accessible to beginning learners should be accomplished in the selection and design of the tasks that accompany them (as opposed to editing or adaptation). Although most applied linguists and teachers agree that bringing such authenticity into the classroom is desirable at some point, one of the major barriers to achieving it is the scarcity of authentic materials that have been analyzed for pedagogical purposes. We were truly delighted to find that so many of our colleagues around the world have been bringing authentic texts into their classrooms and working out innovative ways to use them. We hope our readers will be inspired by their creativity.

Each activity or set of activities in the book centers around an audio, visual, or written text from an English language environment. These include samples from many different television genres, books, magazines, cards, recipes, schedules, brochures, and so on. Each author has provided either a sample of the authentic text she works with or (in the case of copyrighted television) a synopsis of the text and a sample worksheet, if one is used in the lesson.

The activities focus on all the language skills, including reading, writing, grammar, listening, and conversation. The acquisition of cultural knowledge is also a focus of many of the submissions. We have organized the submissions around the media or text types, with reference to the pedagogical aims of each submission in the scholar's margin of each article. We hope that these ideas will inspire and equip others to bring more authenticity into their classrooms.

Ruth E. Larimer
Monterey Institute of
    International Studies
Monterey, California USA

Leigh Schleicher
Minnesota Department of
    Children, Families and Learning
St. Paul, Minnesota USA

References and Further Reading

Biber, D., Conrad, S., & Reppen, R. (1994). Corpus-based approaches to issues in applied linguistics. *Applied Linguistics, 15.*

Cathcart, R. L. (1989). Authentic discourse and survival English curriculum. *TESOL Quarterly, 23,* 105–126.

Swaffar, J. K. (1985). Reading authentic texts in a foreign language: A cognitive model. *Modern Language Journal, 69,*15–34.

Valdman, A. (1992). Authenticity, variation, and communication in the foreign langauge classroom. In C. Kramsch & S. McConnell-Ginet (Eds.), *Text and context.* New York: Heath.

Users' Guide to Activities

Part III: Maps, Mail, and Other Documents

Entertainment and Travel

Consumer Education Through Brochures

Communicating With Cards

Part IV: Texts for Academic and Business Settings

Classroom Talk

Part I: TV, Radio, and Video

Editors' Note

Rich in cultural information, this section explores the use of visual and auditory media in the ESL classroom. Teachers will encounter a variety of ways to access media that go beyond merely checking comprehension to providing a stimulus for language practice using the four skills. The three sections—News and Sports, Advertising, and Entertainment TV—highlight a variety of cultural issues to which international students need exposure. Teachers will see how presentations such as commercials (which actually often annoy native speakers) can be exploited to give inside cultural information to language learners.

◆ News and Sports
Listen With Your Mind

Levels
Intermediate +

Aims
Improve comprehension
of TV news
Develop and use
background knowledge
about news stories and
news programs to
improve listening skills
Practice guessing and
predicting accurately

Class Time
50 minutes the first day;
25–50 minutes the
following 4 days

Preparation Time
20 minutes

Resources
TV and VCR
Videotape
Access to a news
broadcast in English

Television news in English is difficult to understand because broadcasters speak quickly and use technical and idiomatic vocabulary. ESL students need to be made aware of the importance of using background knowledge about news stories and programs when they listen to the news. Because they may not have the background they need, they must learn how to develop it. The strategies of predicting before listening and guessing about what has been heard depend on having background knowledge and being able to use it effectively.

Procedure

1. Record 10 minutes of a TV news broadcast. If possible, choose a portion of the broadcast with several types of discourse: an introduction to the program, headlines, small talk between announcers, news stories, sports, and weather.
   - Day 1 in class, play the tape once without stopping. Ask students to notice which parts of the broadcast are easier or more difficult for them to understand.
   - After watching, have students evaluate their overall percentage of comprehension and mark it on a continuum in their class notebooks:

Sample rating scale				
0%		50%		100%
Comprehension very difficult	difficult	OK	easy	Comprehension very easy

2. Discuss with students which parts of the broadcast were easy, which were difficult, and why. Write their responses on the board. (See Appendix for sample board work.)

3. Explain the terms *top-down* and *bottom-up listening strategies*. Tell students that top-down listening involves using previous background knowledge about news stories, programs, and announcers to predict what they will hear and to help them understand what they hear in a news broadcast. Bottom-up listening involves focusing on the announcer's pronunciation, words, and grammatical structures to understand what he is saying. Both top-down and bottom-up listening strategies are used in most situations, but top-down strategies are especially useful when listening to the news. (For more information on top-down and bottom-up strategies, see Peterson, 1991; Richards, 1990.)

4. Have students watch the news for several days in class. Record the same program every day so that students can build up their background knowledge of the structure of that news broadcast. In the process of watching the news for several days, students will also be building up their content knowledge of the stories currently in the news.

5. Before the students watch the news each day, ask them to predict what they expect to hear, based on their growing background knowledge of news stories. Each day, their predictions about continuing stories should become more specific.

6. After watching the broadcast each day, ask students to mark their percentage of overall comprehension on a continuum like the one above. In this way, students will be able to see their improvement in listening over the week. In addition, have students mark their comprehension of individual stories and rate their background knowledge on each story:

> 3 = a lot of background
> 2 = some background
> 1 = not much background
> 0 = no background

In most cases, students can see that the most difficult stories are those for which they have little or no background knowledge.

7. After watching the same TV news program for 5 days, students will realize that they have developed a lot of background knowledge on stories in the news and on this program you have been watching in class. Elicit from the students how this news program is organized. For example, (a) there is an introduction to the program highlighting important news stories of the day, (b) the two announcers chat and joke, (c) they move to another announcer to get the news, and (d) another person gives the weather report. Discuss how other news programs they are familiar with are organized in a similar or different way.

Caveats and Options

1. Students tend to continue to rely on their bottom-up listening strategies, focusing on pronunciation, vocabulary, and grammar, and they do not utilize their background knowledge. When they have trouble understanding a news story or the small talk between announcers or a weather broadcaster's jokes, direct students to think about the background knowledge they may have about that news story or the organization of the program to help them decide whether this was important information, and if it was, to guess what they think was said. Discuss with students the purpose for listening to the news. Usually we want to know what has happened in a general way and what is new in particular stories we are interested in. Jokes and small talk between announcers are usually not important to us.

2. Have students bring newspapers to class after Day 1. Use newspaper headlines, along with stories students have seen on previous broadcasts, to predict news stories for that day.

3. For homework, have students choose and watch the same news program each day for a week. Ask students to keep a log in which they write about which stories were easiest or most difficult for them to understand, explain why the stories were easy or difficult, and evaluate their comprehension and background knowledge for each story. At the end of the week, they can write about how the program is organized and evaluate their progress in understanding the TV news.

4. For homework, students can read newspaper articles to look for background knowledge on stories they are interested in and do not know much about.
5. Radio news broadcasts may also be used. If possible, start with the TV news to introduce and practice these listening strategies. After a week or so, move to the radio news.
6. It does not violate copyright regulations if you record the news each day and erase it that day after using it in class.

References and Further Reading

Carrell, P. L. (1987). Content and formal schemata in ESL reading. *TESOL Quarterly, 21,* 461–481.

Dunkel, P. (1991). Listening in the native and second/foreign language: Toward an integration of research and practice. *TESOL Quarterly, 25,* 431–457.

Dunkel, P., & Chung, S. C. (1992). The effect of speech modification, prior knowledge, and listening proficiency on EFL lecture learning. *TESOL Quarterly, 25,* 345–374.

Long, D. R. (1989). Second language listening comprehension: A schema-theoretic perspective. *The Modern Language Journal, 73,* 32–40.

Peterson, P. W. (1991). A synthesis of methods for interactive listening. In M. Celce-Murcia (Ed.), *Teaching English as a second or foreign language* (pp. 106–122). Boston: Heinle & Heinle.

Phillips, J. K. (1991). An analysis of text in video newscasts: A tool for schemata building in listeners. In J. Alatis (Ed.), *Georgetown University Round Table on Languages and Linguistics 1991* (pp. 343–367). Washington, DC: Georgetown University Press.

Richards, J. C. (1990). *The language teaching matrix.* Cambridge: Cambridge University Press.

Rost, M. (1990). *Listening in language learning.* New York: Longman.

Weissenrieder, M. (1987). Listening to the news in Spanish. *The Modern Language Journal, 71,* 18–27.

Appendix: Board Work

On Day 1, during the discussion of easy and difficult news stories, it is helpful to arrange students' comments on the chalk- or whiteboard in the following way:

	Bottom-up	Top-down
Difficult	Announcers spoke too fast Announcers used unfamiliar vocabulary (slang, idioms, technical)	I don't know about this story or topic
Easy	Visuals/pictures helped Announcers used easy, common vocabulary	I knew about this story before I've seen this program before I usually watch the news

If students do not mention some of these points, try to elicit them by asking questions, for example: "Which was the most difficult story for you? Why was it difficult? Do you know anything about this story?" If students focus on bottom-up concerns, ask questions about their background knowledge on the topic of the news story.

Do not write the terms *bottom-up* and *top-down* on the board until the end of the discussion when you are ready to explain them to students.

Contributor

Debra Deane is director of the English Language Institute, University of Akron, in the United States, and has taught ESL listening comprehension for 20 years.

You Understand More Than You Think

Levels
High intermediate +

Aims
Recognize ability to catch most of the important content words in radio news broadcasts
Realize that missed words tend to be less important function words
Practice bottom-up listening strategies, focusing on listening for pronunciation, vocabulary, and grammar
Improve understanding of radio news broadcasts

Class Time
20–50 minutes +

Preparation Time
25 minutes

Resources
Radio
Tape recorder and audiotape
Access to a radio news broadcast in English

ESL students often underestimate their listening ability. They attempt to catch every word they hear, and when they miss words, they believe they cannot understand the main ideas. By doing a dictation of a short radio news story and analyzing the types of words that they miss, students can see that, in fact, they are understanding most of the important words and getting the main ideas. They are often surprised to discover how much they actually understand.

Procedure

1. Record a radio news broadcast and choose a story appropriate for the students. A short story of approximately 2–3 minutes is best. Make a copy of the recording for each student.
2. Ask students to listen to the story the first time without stopping the tape. They should try to understand the main ideas of the story.
3. Next, students should replay the story and write each word they hear. They may stop and repeat the tape as often as they like. They should skip lines on their paper as they write the dictation; this will enable them to write in the corrections when they check their dictation with the script. Have students keep track of the amount of time it takes them to do the dictation.
4. Tell students that they are practicing their bottom-up listening strategies, that is, they are focusing on listening for the speaker's pronunciation, vocabulary, and grammar. However, when they miss a word or phrase, they should try to use their background knowledge about the news story and their knowledge of English to guess what the word or phrase might be. They should then write their guessed words in parentheses.

5. After students have finished the dictation, have them estimate the percentage of words they believe they have correct. Then give them a copy of the script. Have students check their own dictation, writing in the corrections on their papers with a different color pen so the corrections are easy to see.

6. Next, give students the Dictation Analysis Work Sheet (see Appendices A and B). It is useful to do this in class so that you can circulate among students and help them categorize their errors into content and function words.

7. Help students use the work sheet to figure out their percentage of comprehension. Students first determine their overall comprehension, then their comprehension of important content words.

8. Students should then compare their percentage of comprehension with their estimate, done prior to checking the dictation. At this point, discuss with students how close they were in their estimate and whether they are under- or overestimating their listening comprehension abilities. For students who are underestimating their listening abilities, encourage them to develop confidence; for students who are overestimating their listening (rare in my experience), encourage them to listen more closely to content words.

Caveats and Options

1. Prior to the dictation activity, students should spend a week or two listening to the news, focusing on the main ideas of the broadcasts and increasing their background knowledge of news stories.

2. Students can do more bottom-up listening dictations throughout the course for homework. When done on a regular basis, students can use the information on the work sheet to see progress in their listening.

3. In addition to radio news, tapes of other authentic discourse can be used. Songs are a good choice because students are often interested in listening to and transcribing them.

4. Dictation is a discrete, intensive listening activity that should not be overused. More time in class should be spent on listening for main ideas in news stories.

References and Further Reading

Anderson, A., & Lynch, T. (1988). *Listening*. Oxford: Oxford University Press.

Brown, G. (1990). *Listening to spoken English* (2nd ed.). New York: Longman.

Davis, P., & Rinvolucri, M. (1988). *Dictation: New methods, new possibilities*. Cambridge: Cambridge University Press.

Dunkel, P. (1991). Listening in the native and second/foreign language: Toward an integration of research and practice. *TESOL Quarterly, 25*, 431–457.

Peterson, P. W. (1991). A synthesis of methods for interactive listening. In M. Celce-Murcia (Ed.), *Teaching English as a second or foreign language* (pp. 106–122). Boston: Heinle & Heinle.

Richards, J. C. (1990). *The language teaching matrix*. Cambridge: Cambridge University Press.

Rost, M. (1990). *Listening in language learning*. New York: Longman.

Weissenrieder, M. (1987). Listening to the news in Spanish. *The Modern Language Journal, 71*, 18-27.

Appendix A: Sample Dictation Analysis Work Sheet, Part 1

Write examples of words you missed in your dictation according to the following categories:

A. Content Words
   1. Names of people:
   2. Names of places:
   3. Unfamiliar words (words you didn't know):
   4. Words you know by sight but misunderstood when listening:
   5. Other (i.e., you're not sure what category they fit in):

B. Function Words/Grammatical Features
   1. Prepositions (e.g., *in, on, at*):
   2. Articles (*a, an, the*):
   3. Auxiliary verbs (e.g., *is, have, did*):
   4. Connecting words (e.g., *and, but, while*):
   5. -*s* ending on verbs or nouns:
   6. -*ed* ending on verbs:
   7. Other:

On the list above, highlight words you missed that you think are necessary to understand this tape.

Appendix B: Sample Dictation Analysis Work Sheet, Part 2

Particular words carry important information that is essential to understand a news story. For example, content words like nouns and verbs, adjectives, and adverbs tell you a lot of information. However, some content words are not necessary to understand the story. For example, names of people and places tell you information but are often not essential. Sometimes it is enough to know that the speaker said a name, but we do not need to catch the specific name.

Function words sometimes carry important information, but often they carry grammatical information that is not essential to understanding the main idea of the story. For example, articles, prepositions, and auxiliary verbs are often not necessary to get the main ideas. Grammatical features are often redundant. For example, we may know that an action is in the past tense because of a time adverb, and so we do not need to hear the -ed ending.

1. What did you estimate as the percentage of words you wrote correctly in this dictation? (before you checked it with the script)

2. Now figure out your percentage of comprehension. There were approximately 350 words in this dictation. (350 is an example for this sample work sheet.) Count the total number of words in your dictation.

   ● Overall comprehension: Count all the content and function words you missed. Write the total here: _____

   Then subtract the number of words you missed from 350 and divide by 350.

   ● Comprehension of important words: Now count *only* the *important* words you highlighted on the list above. Subtract the number of important words you missed from 350 and divide by 350.

3. Compare your percentages of comprehension with your estimate. Were you fairly close in your estimate? If not, explain why you think your estimate was different from your actual percentage of comprehension. How do you feel about your bottom-up listening comprehension ability?

Contributor

Debra Deane is director of the English Language Institute, University of Akron, in the United States and has taught ESL listening comprehension for 20 years.

Read It and Listen to It

Levels
High intermediate

Aims
Use existing reading and
listening skills
Work together to build
new listening, reading,
and vocabulary skills

Class Time
1–3 hours

Preparation Time
1 hour

Resources
Prerecorded television
news clip
TV, VCR, videotape
Local newspaper
Work sheets

Combining video and an article on the same topic reinforces learning. Learning vocabulary is more effective when students have a chance to first read new words and then listen to them. Students who have better listening skills than reading skills may want to begin with a news segment to get the main idea. Students who have better reading than listening skills may want to begin with the reading to get a general understanding of the subject and then view the video.

Procedure

1. Find a newspaper article and corresponding story on television news (see Appendices A and B for samples). Prepare a vocabulary and reading comprehension work sheet for the newspaper article. Prepare a vocabulary and listening comprehension work sheet for the television news item (see Appendices C and D).

2. Give students the newspaper article to read along with the vocabulary and reading comprehension work sheet to do as homework.

3. Have the students check their homework in groups.

4. Distribute the video work sheet with the vocabulary and listening comprehension exercises. Watch the video clip in class.

5. Have the students check the answers on the video work sheet in groups.

6. Do a follow-up to link both exercises such as a general class discussion or a writing assignment to be done at home.

Caveats and Options

1. As students become familiar with the format, have them divide into groups and give them the newspaper article and video clip to prepare. They may want to divide so that they are working on their strength area or they may want to work at preparing an exercise in the area where they have the most difficulty.

2. One follow-up exercise that works well, but is not always readily available, is to use a follow-up video clip about a news story a few days later. Before showing the follow-up story, have the students speculate about the outcome. Give them a list of questions to discuss in groups about a possible outcome, then show the actual video clip (see Appendix E). This exercise is especially popular because different groups invariably come up with different outcomes and then are surprised at the authentic outcome.

3. This kind of exercise works best with human interest stories or with stories in which the focus is on some kind of problem rather than on mainstream international news.

4. The order can be switched so that students first watch the video and do the work sheet, and then read the article and do the work sheet.

Appendix A: Sample Newspaper Article

Clinton announces US recognition of Vietnam

President says his wartime past was not a factor

By John Aloysius Farrell
GLOBE STAFF

WASHINGTON – President Clinton, vowing to move beyond "the haunting and painful past," and fight through economic engagement for the ideals of freedom that were lost on the battlefield two decades ago, extended full diplomatic relations to Vietnam yesterday.

"Let the future be our destination," a solemn Clinton told a hushed crowd in the East Room of the White House. "This moment offers us the opportunity to bind up our own wounds. They have resisted time for too long."

Clinton's decision was criticized by some POW-MIA activists, veterans groups and congressional foes, but drew warm applause from a large contingent of Republican and Democratic lawmakers, Vietnam veterans, business leaders and diplomats who packed the ballroom.

Clinton, once an antiwar protester who avoided military service during the war, told reporters before the ceremony that his own experience and political fate had not entered into his decision, nor made it more difficult. "None ... no," he said.

Sen. John McCain, the Republican from Arizona who spent more than five years as a POW in North Vietnam and has given Clinton political cover on the issue, said the president's past made yesterday's announcement "an act that required some courage."

"I applaud the president's decision," McCain said. "I believe very strongly that the American people will approve of this move, that this issue will recede, and hopefully we can help those people who are less fortunate than I, who still have difficulty coming back from Vietnam."

The Socialist Republic of Vietnam is expected to move quickly to exchange ambassadors and open embassies. Secretary of State Warren M. Christopher will visit Vietnam in August, Clinton said, to discuss these and other matters.

Vietnam's Prime Minister Vo Van Kiet appeared on nationwide television and pledged continued efforts to account fully for Americans missing from the war. "These relations will serve the interests of the two peoples and contribute to the cause of peace and stability in the region and the world," he said.

Clinton said that good relations and trade terms will depend on Vietnam's continued cooperation in the search for missing American servicemen from the Vietnam War, and that normalization is the best route toward resolving the POW-MIA issue.

Clinton's critics, however, said the administration had caved in under pressure from US corporate interests that want to compete in Vietnamese markets.

"The Vietnamese have not given us all the information they can unilaterally provide on our POWs and MIAs, and now the president has given away all the leverage we have by rewarding communist Vietnam with official recognition," said Sen. Bob Smith, a Republican from New Hampshire. "Attempts to normalize relations with Vietnam is putting profit over principle."

Smith said he will join Senate Majority Leader Robert Dole of Kansas, GOP Sen. Jesse Helms of North Carolina and other lawmakers in attempts to cut off funding for an embassy or ambassador in Vietnam. The American Legion opposes normalization, as does the National League of Families, the leading POW-MIA organization.

"This is an issue of national honor, and the president has today dishonored the families and veterans who sacrificed in Vietnam," said Smith.

Indeed, some of the POW-MIA family members who met with Clinton before he made his announcement declined to stay for the White House ceremony, showing displeasure by their boycott.

"They pledged to stay involved and to work with us. That is not to say that they, all of them, agreed with this decision," National Security Adviser Anthony Lake said.

But Sen. Robert Kerrey, a Democrat from Nebraska who received the Congressional Medal of Honor after losing a leg in Vietnam, hailed Clinton's decision.

"The president pays less of a political price any time he does what he did today, which is say, 'I'm going to do the right thing and I don't really give a damn what the polls say.' And he did the right thing today," Kerrey said.

"We went to Vietnam to fight for freedom, but the war was corrupted," Kerrey said. "Today we are saying it's desirable to keep on fighting for freedom in a peaceful fashion."

Kerrey said he and other Vietnam veterans in the Senate would oppose any efforts by Dole or others to cut off funds for an embassy.

"They're wrong. I intend to fight them. It's wallowing in the past," Kerrey said. "For Bob Dole or anybody else who wants to get up and try to score a political point, they're going to face people like me who say 'Shame on you.'"

Sen. John F. Kerry, a Democrat from Massachusetts whose role as chairman of a Senate POW-MIA committee helped pave the way for yesterday's announcement, said "Vietnam is too strategic an asset to ignore" and can act as a foreign policy counterweight to China and other nations in the region.

The economic stakes are high as well. Kerry said. Vietnam, with 73 million people, is the 13th biggest country in the world, has untapped oil reserves, and is in dire need of new highways, telecommunications systems, public utilities and financial investment.

Clinton made his announcement while flanked on a small stage by McCain, Kerry, Kerrey, Vice President Al Gore, Sen. Charles Robb, Democrat of Virginia, and other Vietnam veterans. Republican Sens. Alan Simpson of Wyoming and Robert Bennett of Utah were in the audience, signs of the bipartisan support with which the administration believes it can defeat Smith's attempts to cut off funding.

"Whatever we may think about the political decisions of the Vietnam era, the brave Americans who fought and died there had noble motives," Clinton said. "They fought for the freedom and independence of the Vietnamese people. Today the Vietnamese are independent, and we believe this step will help to extend the reach of freedom in Vietnam.

"This step will also help our own country to move forward on an issue that has separated Americans from one another for too long," Clinton said. "Whatever divided us before, let us consign to the past. Let this moment, in the words of the Scripture, be a time to heal and a time to build."

President Clinton, accompanied at the White House by legislative supporters, announces the extension of diplomatic relations to Vietnam.

Reprinted courtesy of *The Boston Globe*. Used with permission.

Appendix B: Sample News Program Synopses

U.S. Recognition of Vietnam

Synopsis of ABC News, July 15, 1995

The report starts out as a review of the history of events that led up to U.S. involvement. There are scenes from the film archives that show how prevalent the war was in the news during the 1960s and 1970s. The reporter states how the United States got involved to prevent the communists from taking over, or that was the line that four presidents fed the American people. There is also mention of how the war divided the American people as it became increasingly clear that we were involved in a battle in a country that did not wish for our intervention. The memorial is important because it showed how we are finally letting go and moving on.

Synopsis of CBS News, July 15, 1995

The report is a review of President Clinton's speech at the opening of the memorial. The report focuses on the context and perspective "why now?" According to the report, the most important implication is for President Clinton's reelection. The report also brings out the economic implications of reestablishing relations with Vietnam. The pros and cons of economic involvement are shown in some detail.

Appendix C: Sample Newspaper Work Sheet on Vocabulary

Directions: Circle the letter of the word or phrase that most closely matches the underlined word or phrase in meaning.

1. President Clinton <u>vowed</u> to move ahead.

   a. happened   b. promised   c. opposed

2. Some family members of missing military personnel <u>declined</u> to stay for the White House ceremony.

   a. lowered   b. decided   c. refused

3. The <u>hushed</u> crowd was supportive of President Clinton's decision.

   a. loud   b. secretive   c. silent

4. The decision by the President was opposed by his <u>foes</u>.

   a. friends   b. opponents   c. colleagues

5. On the other hand, a large <u>contingent</u> of Republican and Democratic lawmakers were supportive of his decision.

   a. disproportionate   b. representative   c. normal
      group   group   group

6. The <u>packed</u> ballroom contained lawmakers from both parties, Vietnam veterans, business leaders and diplomats.

   a. crowded   b. wrapped   c. fitted

7. McCain hopes that the issue will <u>recede</u>.

   a. advance   b. reoccur   c. fade

8. Vo Van Kiet <u>pledged</u> to continue efforts to account for Americans still missing from the war.

   a. promised   b. forgot   c. paid

9. Their absence was a <u>boycott</u> to show their disapproval of the President's decision.

   a. admission   b. protest   c. abstention

10. It was a <u>solemn</u> President Clinton who talked to the crowd in the ballroom.

   a. happy   b. relaxed   c. serious

11. Some critics believe that the Vietnamese have not <u>unilaterally</u> provided as much information to Americans as they could have.

   a. onesidedly   b. single-handedly   c. faithfully

12. Senator Robert Kerrey does not think that opposing politicians should <u>wallow</u> in the past, but rather embrace the move forward by President Clinton.

   a. revel   b. forget   c. regret

Appendix D: Sample Newspaper Work Sheet

Reading Comprehension

Directions: Answer each of the following questions based on information found in the text.

1. Why did President Clinton want to reestablish diplomatic relations with Vietnam?
2. What group has been critical of the President's decision and why?
3. What was President Clinton's position during the time the war was going on? How has that position influenced his current decision?
4. How does Senator John McCain feel about the President's decision? Why is his opinion important?
5. What are some outcomes that Americans are hoping for?
6. Explain Senator Bob Smith's statement, "Attempts to normalize relations with Vietnam is putting profit over principle."
7. How did POW-MIA families react to the news?
8. How does Senator Robert Kerrey feel about the President's decision? Why is his opinion important?
9. How is Vietnam a strategic asset we can't ignore?

Appendix E: Sample Video Work Sheet

ABC News, July 13, 1995

Vocabulary: Make sure you understand these words and idioms as they are used in context.

- *dominate*
- *despots*
- *hang on to*
- *heed*
- *wounds*
- *magnet*

Listening Comprehension

Background
1. How did Vietnam dominate American life in the 1960s and 1970s?
2. Why were Americans in Vietnam during this time period?
3. Who were the colonial masters in the 19th century in Vietnam?
4. Which lesson did Americans not heed from these former masters?
5. How many Americans died in the war?
6. Which presidents were involved during the war?

Current Situation
1. Which well-known war veteran helped President Clinton by supporting his decision to reestablish ties with Vietnam?
2. Give three reasons why the President wants to reestablish relations with Vietnam now.
3. Whose support is most important to President Clinton?
4. What's in Vietnam for Americans?
5. How could investment by American companies hurt Americans at home?

Discussion
1. Why do you think the United States remained involved in the war so long when it was clear that it was losing?
2. Why are Americans mixed in their reaction to President Clinton's move to reestablish diplomatic ties with Vietnam?

Contributor

Virginia Drislane teaches ESL in the Harvard Intensive English Language program and at the Center for English Language and Orientation Program, at Boston University, in the United States. She also does market research for companies around Boston.

◆ Advertising

Language and Culture in 25 Seconds

Levels
Intermediate

Aims
Practice prediction and
listening skills
Become exposed to
authentic language and
culture found in
television commercials

Class Time
30–40 minutes

Preparation Time
1 hour

Resources
Television commercial
from an
English-speaking
country
TV and VCR
Copies of the
commercial dialogue
Work sheet for watching
commercials

Students want and need exposure to samples of everyday authentic language and culture presented in a very visually stimulating format. Television commercials, with their 25-second barrage of language and culture, are an excellent source. Commercials are short, focused slices of contemporary society—music, clothing, family relationships—and colloquial English that are often more manageable in length for teaching than other video materials.

Procedure

1. Record an appropriate TV commercial, and transcribe the dialogue.
2. Previewing: Divide the class up into groups of three or four students. Write the product and its name on the board (e.g., Pepsi) and ask students to write down five things they expect to hear (e.g., the sound of a can opening, someone saying, "Pepsi is the best") and five things they expect to see (e.g., a Pepsi can, a famous sports figure promoting the product) on their work sheet (see Appendix A). Write some of the student responses on the board.
3. Viewing: Play the tape with the sound off. Ask students to check their predictions by circling the ones they see on their work sheets. Pause the tape as needed to allow students time to process what they see. Then ask students to revise or add any items in a second list based on the visual images they just saw. Have students act out what they think the people are saying in the commercial. Often this allows students to generate ideas more freely and spontaneously in a relaxed and enjoyable setting.

4. Watch the commercial again with the sound turned up and have students listen to the content of the commercial. This time, ask students to check which words, phrases, sentences, and sounds they hear and compare this to the list on their papers and on the board.

5. Postviewing: Give students a copy of the transcript of the commercial with some of the words deleted. Have them try to predict (or recall) the words which are missing before listening again and write these words in the dialogue. Then play the commercial and ask students to fill in the missing words.

6. Watch the commercial again, taking notes of any facial expressions, body movements (gestures), culture-specific paralanguage (e.g., the hesitation pause, *uh . . . , or uh-huh* as a sign of affirmation or acknowledgment in English), communication patterns, stereotypes, or unique advertising techniques they notice.

7. Write these ideas on the board and discuss how these points of culture are similar to or different from those of their native cultures. Ask students to give specific examples, if possible.

Caveats and Options

1. Tell students to write down whether they agree or disagree with the advertiser's claims. This gives higher level students the opportunity to enhance their critical thinking skills by analyzing the cultural content of the commercial.

2. Have students role-play the dialogue or have students create their own original commercial based on the same product complete with authentic realia, props, and background music. Videotape the predictions and have students select the "Commercial of the Year" based on originality, language use, special effects, humor, and emotional impact.

3. Pedagogically speaking, the most effective commercials tend to be ones that (a) tell or narrate a story through multiple images; (b) have characters who express emotions verbally or using body language, providing linguistic clues to fill gaps in understanding; (c) target the students' age groups through popular culture references (e.g., music, clothing, dance, sports); and (d) coincide closely with language skills and academic content currently being covered in class.

4. Remember that commercials can be adapted to review almost any language skill. Don't bother spending fruitless hours looking for one that is replete with examples of the past perfect progressive.

References and Further Reading

Davis, R. D. (1994/1995, December/January). Commercial messages: You got the right one, baby! *TESOL Matters*, p. 10.

Stempleski, S., & Tomalin, B. (1990). *Video in action: Recipes for using video in language teaching*. London: Prentice-Hall International.

Appendix A: Sample Commercial Synopsis and Viewing Work Sheet

The following synopsis is of a commercial that used images from the movie *Field of Dreams,* starring Kevin Costner.

The commercial begins in a baseball field in the middle of a cornfield with a young man (representing Ray Kinsella in the movie) sitting on the sideline bleachers looking at a baseball card of his deceased father and obviously longing for the past. Suddenly, the camera shifts to the outfield where the young man's father suddenly emerges from the cornfield; the two walk toward each other, exchanging warm greetings and reminiscing about the "good old days." The father then asks for a drink, expecting a Pepsi, but his son pulls out a generic cola brand (Fred's Cola) from the cooler and throws it to his father. The father looks at the can and, with a very disappointed look, exclaims, "This isn't a Pepsi!" The younger man, however, proudly responds with a wide grin, "I know. I saved nine cents," but is shocked when his father throws it right back to him, and then walks back into the cornfield saying, "Unbelievable. The boy saved a lousy nine cents."

Name _____

Commercial _____

1. Write five things you think you will see in the commercial. Write five things you think you will hear (e.g., words, phrases, sounds) in the commercial.

2. Take note of any of the following items you see in the commercial: facial expressions, gestures, body movement, sounds, humor, stereotypes, similarities/differences in advertising in your country.
3. What group(s) are the advertisers trying to attract? Children? Teenagers? Young adults? Middle aged? Senior citizens? Housewives? Retired? Business people? College students? Male? Female? Other?
4. Critical thinking: Do you believe the advertiser's claims? Why or why not?

Contributors

Randall S. Davis teaches at Nagoya City University in Japan and specializes in using video, comic strips, and simulation games in the classroom. Michael Furmanovsky uses documentaries, commercials, and other authentic video materials to teach language and American Studies at Kobe University, Japan.

Guess the Advertisement

Levels
Intermediate +

Aims
Practice specific
listening skills and using
descriptive language
Consider media culture
in the target culture and
compare it with own
culture

Class Time
1 hour

Preparation Time
10 minutes plus
recording time

Resources
TV and VCR
Videotaped
advertisements
Work sheet

Students are often told to watch TV in order to improve their language skills. Because advertisements make up a large part of air time, it would seem appropriate to utilize this form of authentic material as much as possible. Advertisements convey a lot of information about the cultural aspects of a society. They can also be extremely wacky and thus useful to stimulate discussion.

Procedure

1. Engage students in a discussion using the questions in the Appendix.
2. Ask the students to break into two groups: One group will watch the TV advertisement with no sound while the other group sits facing them with their backs to the TV. The organization for this activity will depend on how many TVs and VCRs are available.
3. Ask the students viewing the advertisement to describe to their partners, who are facing them, what they see.
4. Ask the students who cannot see the TV to listen carefully to the description and fill in the second column of the table (i.e., the description of the advertisement).
5. Next, the students who took notes should offer two or three guesses as to what is being advertised (see Column 3).
6. Then, ask all the students to watch the advertisement together, with sound, to check how much detail was noted. Fill out Column 2 of another identical work sheet, adding detail.
7. Ask the students to discuss in small groups how the product or similar products are advertised in their country, and to fill out Column 4 on the work sheet.

Caveats and Options

1. The activity can be done using printed advertisements instead of taped ones.
2. The activity could be organized into a competitive game whereby groups have to guess what is being advertised.
3. A follow-up to this kind of activity is project work. Different groups of students could focus on advertisements that use a particular group or part of society to sell their products (e.g., products sold using a particular animal or children or women). A collection of advertisements listed under various categories could provide excellent opportunities for discussion about culture, stereotyping, who watches TV, and so on.
4. The students could be asked to design an advertisement for a certain product. The judging could also be undertaken by students and a small prize offered to the winner.

Appendix: Sample Commercial Synopsis and Work Sheet

Synopsis of sample ad for "Dental White" tooth polish

Dental White is a new formula that promises to whiten dirty, stained teeth. The product is introduced by a famous female celebrity who demonstrates the quality of the product by referring to, and showing shots of, everyday people, ranging from a young woman to a construction worker to a mature lady. The product is professed to be the equivalent of an expensive dentist's treatment at a fraction of the price. Enticing benefits include a money-back guarantee, a refund if the customer is not happy, and a buy-now-and-receive-a- double-sized-bottle offer.

Preview Questions

1. What makes a good advertisement?
2. Have you ever bought a product after having seen an advertisement for it? Were you influenced by the advertisement? In what way?

Sample Work Sheet (filled in after hearing version with sound)

	Description of advertisement	Product	Advertised in your culture
Ad 1	● famous American celebrity talking about a cream which cleans teeth ● promises to make you more beautiful and attractive ● shows examples of people with very white teeth (men and women) ● includes a scientific explanation of how it works ● refund if you are not happy	Dental White	This section would obviously depend upon which country the students are from. It would be very interesting in a multi-cultural group to discuss how different products are advertised, focusing on issues such as: ● images of men and women ● roles of men, women, young, and old people ● gender ● image of beauty

Contributor

Sue Fitzgerald is a lecturer at the English Language Study-Centre of Hong Kong Polytechnic, Hong Kong.

Good Parents Choose . . .

Levels
Intermediate +

Aims
Focus listening compre-
hension to identify
product slogan
Think critically in order
to identify target audi-
ence and type of appeal
Discuss, compare, and
contrast cultural values
mirrored in TV
advertisements

Class Time
1–2 hours

Preparation Time
1 hour

Resources
Magazines appealing to
different audiences
Scissors and post-it notes
(or flags)
10–15 TV advertisements
from various time slots
to get a variety of target
audiences and products
Sample magazine
advertisements handout
TV, VCR, remote control

TV advertisements are useful for building cultural awareness because they provide clues to gender roles, social values, and interpersonal relationships. They can also provide an introduction to persuasive appeals useful in persuasive writing and can build a greater awareness of target audiences.

Procedure

1. Show students two or three advertisements (see Appendix A) that use different techniques to appeal to the target audience (e.g., cruise advertisement appeals to desire for the good life; restaurant ad appeals to desire for happy relationship). Discuss target audiences (e.g., moms, dads, children, career women, single men) and list choices on chalkboard. Also identify the slogan for each product.
2. Give each pair of students a magazine and ask them to select several advertisements, marking each with a flag so the ads can be found again easily. Orient students to Handout 1 (see Appendix B) and ask them to list target audience and type of appeal. When finished, ask them to put their handout inside the magazine and to trade with another pair of students.
3. The pair of students receiving the magazine are to read the type of appeal and target audience and decide which advertisement goes with which appeal and audience, then complete Handout 1 by filling in the page number, slogan, and type of product. They then group with the other pair to check their work.
4. Work as a class to brainstorm a list on the chalkboard of types of appeals that can be used. Possibilities could include appeals to fun, attractiveness, luxury, safety, adventure, health, strength/virility, being a good parent, a good wife, or any others that interest the class.

5. Orient students to Handout 2 (see Appendix C) and tell them they will be viewing a TV advertisement. They will view the ad once to identify product and target audience, then view a second time to identify/write the slogan and the type of appeal used. Practice together with the first advertisement.

6. Play the next advertisement twice and give students time to fill out Handout 2 and to ask questions. Check answers and then tell them that you will show three ads in a row before viewing the second time, so they will need to listen and write quickly in order to keep up. Debrief and again show three in a row to complete the viewing.

7. Put students into groups of four or five students and ask them to compare answers and to circle any on which they disagree. Browse, answer questions, and see which ones most of the class had trouble with for further debriefing as a class.

8. Ask students to stay in their groups and to discuss cultural values reflected in the advertisements. For example, does the society portrayed value older people? Are women expected to have careers? Is there an emphasis on consumerism? Is the society nationalistic? Religious? Is it mostly urban or rural?

9. For a homework assignment, ask the students to compare the culture with their own culture and to write a journal entry comparing at least three values identified in the advertisements with values in the home society.

Caveats and Options

1. Step 1 can also be used to introduce the topic, with Step 2 conducted as an individual homework assignment in which students will be asked to bring in their own magazine from home.

2. Step 5, after practice, could also be conducted as a class game, with students working in teams to listen for the correct slogan and write it correctly on the chalkboard. Teams could be divided into subgroups (e.g., "dictionary" group to look up words for correct spelling of the slogan, "think" groups to decide target audience and product, and a "checker" group to find errors).

3. Step 9 could also be adapted to an independent (challenge) listening/writing activity in which students listen to two TV advertisements at home and compare and contrast the ads on the basis of (a) values

promoted or displayed, (b) appeals used for specific target audiences, and (c) an analysis as to how effective they think the two ads are and why.

References and Further Reading

Schrank, J. (1987). The language of advertising claims. In T. K. Anderson & K. Forrester (Eds.), *Point counterpoint* (pp. 153–161). New York: Harcourt, Brace, Jovanovich.

Appendix A: Magazine Advertisement

Used with permission.

Used with permission.

Appendix B: Sample Handout 1

Examples of Target Audience:

single men
fathers
mothers
married women
career women
older couples

Examples of Types of Appeals:

luxury
safety
health
sex appeal
adventure
belonging

Directions

Part 1

Work with your partner to choose five advertisements from the magazine you have been given. Mark each on the side with a flag so you can find it again easily. For each ad, decide (a) who the target audience is and (b) what type of appeal is used (see lists above if needed). Fill in target audience and type of appeal on the chart below, mixing the order of the ads. Do not fill in the rest of the information.

Advertisement page no. and product	Advertisement slogan	Target audience	Type of appeal
_____	_____	_____	_____
_____	_____	_____	_____
_____	_____	_____	_____
_____	_____	_____	_____
_____	_____	_____	_____

Part 2

Now trade with another pair. Read the target audience and type of appeal listed, look at the advertisements, and fill in your "best guess" as to the advertisement page number, product, and the slogan used. When you finish, get together and see if you were right.

Appendix C: Sample Handout 2

Directions: Watch the TV ads and try to decide what the product is. Who is the target audience? List your answers in the chart below. Watch and listen a second time and identify/write the slogan and the type of appeal used. You will do the first one together to practice.

Product	Target Audience	Slogan	Type of Appeal Used

Contributor

Kim Hughes Wilhelm, International English Program curriculum coordinator at Southern Illinois University-Carbondale, has taught ESL and foreign language in the United States and ESL/EFL in Hong Kong and Malaysia.

◆ Entertainment TV
The Kiss Hello

Levels
Beginning–intermediate

Aims
Explore greetings
Observe current and
popular North American
sitcom humor
Understand North
American cultural rules
for greetings and
leave-takings

Class Time
1 hour

Preparation Time
1 hour

Resources
TV and VCR
Videotape of Seinfeld
episode "The Kiss Hello"
(1994–1995 season) or
any set of sitcom clips
focusing on a speech
act or certain type of
situation
Video work sheet

S tudents need and want to comprehend current North American humor as well as make comparisons between the customs and humor of different cultures. This activity is appropriate for any classroom dealing with North American customs, humor, or relationships. Any current sitcom episode or series of clips from an episode dealing with family life and relationships, greetings, and closings will work well (you just have to be willing to watch a lot of TV programs as you prepare).

Procedure

1. Locate Seinfeld episode "Kiss Hello" (or another episode) on video and cue up clips that illustrate how people greet each other.
2. Prepare handout for students (see Appendix A).
3. Discuss greetings in other cultures and countries as a whole group or in small student groups.
4. Brainstorm list and put on board or poster paper.
5. Play video clips for class without volume.
6. Have students complete the handout.
7. Ask students to share ideas as a whole class or in pairs.
8. Play each separate clip again with sound (as many times as students wish).
9. Have students self-check answers and ideas.
10. Discuss ways of greeting and summarize video clips and storyline.

Caveats and Options

1. Try videotaping openings and greetings from a variety of sitcoms. Discuss the different ways Americans typically greet each other given the various examples.

2. The instructor can make this activity more grammar-oriented by creating a cloze test from the dialogue in the episodes.

3. Students love video and current North American humor, lifestyles, and culture. Adding such an activity to the classroom repertoire is refreshing and fun. The end result need not be a piece of writing; discussing and retelling the story keeps students engaged in the learning process.

References and Further Reading

Connell, E. L., Lewis, M., Turner, J., Kling, J., & Tickle, A. (1995, March). *Building a content-based program: A dynamic dialogue*. Colloquium presented at the 29th Annual TESOL Convention, Long Beach, CA.

Connell, E. L., & Partch, P. (1995, January). *Reality bites: Adapting authentic materials into comprehensible chunks*. Workshop at Steinbeck Regional CATESOL Conference, Monterey, CA.

Appendix A: Synopsis and Sample Work Sheet

We will watch a series of six or seven very short video clips from the popular TV show "Seinfeld." First, we will view the clips without sound. Each clip tells part of a whole story.

Synopsis: In this Seinfeld episode, Jerry is obsessed with not kissing females hello (European style of greeting) because it makes him feel uncomfortable. At the same time, Kramer has launched a "friendliness" campaign in the apartment building, sensing that tenants need to know each other's names and faces in order to live harmoniously. What ensues, of course, is Jerry's avoidance of the expected greeting ritual and, thus, everyone in the building turns against him.

Vocabulary
- *kiss hello*
- *Klondike bar*
- *kiss hello program*
- *mushroomed*
- *defaced*
- *to admire*

1. Can you guess what is happening in each clip? Can you guess the relationship between the people in each clip?

    Video Clip 1:

    Video Clip 2:

    Video Clip 3:

    Video Clip 4:

    Video Clip 5:

    Video Clip 6:

    Video Clip 7:

2. Can you explain how Americans like/don't like to greet each other? Is it the same in your country?

Contributor

Eve L. Connell is a public speaking and business English specialist and teacher trainer for the MA programs at the Monterey Institute of International Studies, as well as an ESL Instructor at Monterey Peninsula College, in the United States.

Discuss Among Yourselves

Levels
High intermediate +

Aims
Focus on examples of
frequently used
discussion strategies
Practice using these
skills by producing a
talk show
View selves during a
discussion and
self-evaluate language
behavior

Class Time
3 hours

Preparation Time
Several hours

Resources
Viewing class: Tape of a
talk show, VCR and
monitor, work sheet
Taping class: VCR (with
plug-in microphone)
and blank tape
Evaluating class:
Evaluation form

Critics might compare the immense popularity of talk shows in the United States to the American love of junk food: Both tastes are satisfied by an overwhelming variety of choices, many of which seem overly self-indulgent. On second look, however, talk shows can be seen to have both social and educational worth. A window on popular culture, talk shows often focus on values, norms, and behavior and can demonstrate to students how people in the United States often interact—exploring a topic by engaging in discussion with others. Through creating and participating in a talk show, students practice and become more comfortable using discussion skills. This is of particular importance to students who will study in the United States or use English in professional situations.

Procedure

Part 1: Viewing the Talk Show

1. Record and preview a talk show.
2. Determine how to segment the video to allow for comprehension checks.
3. Prepare a work sheet including essential vocabulary, idioms and focus or discrete listening questions, depending on your objectives (see Appendix A).
4. Find out who has seen talk shows in their country or in the United States and talk about typical subject matter or guests. Also talk about the role of the talk show host.
5. Distribute work sheet and review vocabulary and focus questions, telling students that the purpose of the activity is to work on discussion skills.

6. Students should form pairs or small groups to complete the work sheet after viewing each segment of the video.
7. Play the video, pausing after each segment to check comprehension, replaying if necessary, and allowing students to discuss and answer questions.
8. Discuss students' answers, particularly those dealing with discussion skills: questioning techniques and types of responses.
9. Discuss the cultural aspects of what was discussed and how.

Part 2: Creating Student Talk Shows

1. Tell students they will next create a talk show in order to practice the discussion skills they've just observed. Divide students into groups of four or five.
2. Tell students in each group to agree upon a topic that is likely to evoke many different opinions/reactions. Students then designate a talk show host and guest roles.
3. Make sure students have chosen what seems to be a viable topic, then tell each student to prepare an open-ended question related to the topic that other students could answer. They should not reveal their question to the others.

Part 3: Filming the Student Talk Shows

1. Have students make a stage, with chairs formed in a semicircle.
2. Groups will take turns "airing" their talk shows, with each group first writing their topic and questions on the board or big sheets of paper for all to see. Have the class correct or improve the questions.
3. Establish a time limit for each talk show (10–15 minutes) and show students how to use the microphone.
4. Decide how the audience (other class members) should participate.
5. Tape each group's show. If possible, tape all shows during one class period.

Part 4: Viewing of Students' Talk Shows

1. Prepare an evaluation form (see Appendix B).
2. With students in their talk show groups again, distribute the form and have them evaluate others' talk show discussions as well as their own.
3. The teacher should also fill out an evaluation form for each group.
4. Review evaluations then return to the groups to read.

Caveats and Options

1. Choose a show in which you can observe many conversation strategies at work (e.g., follow-ups, probing, summarizing, restating, hypothesizing, avoidance).
2. You will probably want to introduce and practice these strategies in class before doing this activity (see References).
3. You could suggest topics or provide a list for students to choose from (see References).
4. It is helpful for talk show participants to be able to read their questions during the show, so the chalkboard or big posters should act as cue cards.
5. Class members in the audience could be allowed to ask guests additional questions.
6. You could use the evaluation form to comment on pronunciation.
7. Encourage students to take on character roles for fun or to depersonalize their behavior or answers.

References and Further Reading

Kehe, D., & Dustin Kehe, P. (1994). *Conversation strategies: Pair and group activities for developing communicative competence*. Brattleboro, VT: Pro Lingua Associates.

Zelman, N. E. (1986). *Conversation inspirations for ESL*. Brattleboro, VT: Pro Lingua Associates.

Appendix A: Student Work Sheet for Talk Show Viewing

Talk Show:	The Montel Williams Show
Topic:	Parent/Teenager Control
Synopsis:	Participants and viewers of this hour-long program are asked to consider the issue of parent-teenager control. The question is: "How far should parents go to find out what their teenager is doing?" Three sets of parents and their teenage daughters describe their experiences, offering a variety of perspectives on the issue. Montel circulates among the audience eliciting reactions and inviting questions for the guests. He attempts to control the turn-taking and interrupting, while commenting and asking follow-up and clarification type questions. He frequently plays devil's advocate by hypothesizing and challenging people's answers. After the featured guests have told their stories, a consultant from a teen marketing firm is brought on to give her opinion about the way the parents have handled these situations. There is some back-and-forth conversation between the consultant, the guests, and Montel. Finally, Montel closes the show by summarizing the main points made during the show and giving his personal advice to parents.

1. Previewing
   Discuss the following terms and predict their relationship to the topic:
   ● *private investigator*
   ● *curfew*
   ● *hang out*
   ● *to sue*
   ● *undercover*
   Discuss the following:
   ● How much should parents control their teenagers?
   ● When is a child "on his own" to make decisions?
   ● Should teenagers have a curfew? In what situations?
   ● How should parents handle a disobedient teenager?

2. Viewing
   Segment 1: Discussion Strategies
   Find examples of the following:

3. Interrupting
   - Who is involved:
   - What they said and did:

4. Summarizing
   - Who is involved:
   - What they said and did:

5. Comprehension
   Discuss the following in small groups:
   - What is the problem according to this 16-year-old? According to her mother?
   - How is she similar or different from a 16-year-old in your culture?
   - What did her mother do to her? Did her mother have a right to do this?
   - What do you think her mother's motivation was?

   Segment 2: Discussion Strategies
   Find examples of the following:

   Follow-up question
   - Who is involved:
   - What they said and did:

6. Hypothesizing
   - Who is involved:
   - What they said and did:

7. Comprehension
   Discuss the following in small groups:
   - What is the problem in this situation, according to the mother? the daughter?

● Why did the mother do this?
● Would you do any of the things this mother did to your child? Why or why not?

Segment 3: Discussion Strategies
Find examples of the following:

8. Soliciting another's opinion
   ● Who is involved:
   ● What they said and did:

9. Clarifying
   ● Who is involved:
   ● What they said and did:

10. Comprehension
    Discuss the following in small groups:
    ● What have the parents done in this situation?
    ● Do you think these are responsible parents?
    ● How could the parents have handled the situation differently?

Appendix B: Evaluation Form for Student Talk Shows

Talk Show participants: _____

I. Discussion Strategies used: (check all that apply)

_____ follow-up questions   Who:

_____ clarifications   Who:

_____ summarizing   Who:

_____ interrupting   Who:

_____ agreeing   Who:

_____ disagreeing   Who:

_____ hypothesizing   Who:

_____ soliciting an opinion   Who:

_____ confirming   Who:

_____ avoiding a question   Who:

II. Voice and Body Language (comment on individual students as appropriate):

1. Volume

   Excellent   Good   Needs Improvement

   Comment:

2. Speed

   Excellent   Good   Needs Improvement

   Comment:

3. Intonation

   Excellent   Good   Needs Improvement

   Comment:

4. Clarity (Pronunciation)

   Excellent   Good   Needs Improvement

   Comment:

5. Gestures

   Excellent   Good   Needs Improvement

   Comment:

6. Eye Contact

   Excellent   Good   Needs Improvement

   Comment:

Contributor

Kristi J. Newgarden teaches in the intensive English studies program at Kansai Gaidai University, in Osaka, Japan.

Telling It Play by Play

Levels
Advanced

Aims
Explore how the simple present tense is used to convey present action Observe and analyze verb tense usage at a discourse level Recognize how one tense form can be used for a variety of functions

Class Time
30–90 minutes

Preparation Time
2 hours if you record and transcribe own sports broadcast; 30–40 minutes if you record prepared transcript

Resources
Audiotaped sports broadcast
Student handout
Video clips of exciting sports events (optional)

This activity is designed to explore linguistic features of sports broadcast speech, with a special focus on the use of the simple present tense in play-by-play coverage.

Procedure

1. Begin by asking the students to describe an exciting moment in sports that they have seen on television or heard on the radio. Ask them to talk about how the television or radio commentators narrated the action (on the field, on the court) for the viewers or listeners.
2. Ask students to listen to the taped broadcast segments of a football game. Ask them to guess what is happening on the field for each play. Tell students to indicate on their work sheets where the ball is and to list other actions taking place for each play (see Appendix A).
3. Have the students listen again and write all the verbs that they hear. Encourage the students to work with other students and pool their responses.
4. Distribute copies of the broadcast transcript to the students (see Appendix B). Ask them to locate the verbs and to note that many of the verbs are in the simple present. Ask the students to discuss why present tense is effective for broadcast language. Suggested discussion questions: What effect does the present tense create during the actual play? Does the play feel exciting or more real?
5. Next, ask small groups of students to role play a broadcast of a sports event. They can think of their own sports event, or you may play video clips of exciting sports moments to prompt the students. Play the video clips without the sound and allow the students to create their own commentary.

6. Depending on the class level and interests, you may want to record and discuss how effective the students' broadcasts are.

1. This lesson presumes a certain degree of familiarity with the game of football. Depending on the class population, students may find it interesting to learn the rules and vocabulary specific to a sport. If possible, choose broadcasts for sports with which your class is already familiar.

Caveats and Options

Acknowledgments

The artwork is by the contributor. Radio broadcast used with permission of the broadcaster, John Chapman-Rienstra.

Appendix A: Student Work Sheet

A. You will hear a broadcast of a football game between The Ohio State University and the University of Michigan. For each play, indicate where you think the ball is on the field. Take notes on what you think is happening during each play. Compare your notes with those of your classmates.

Hint: Michigan quarterback Griese's name is pronounced [gree-see]); Michigan running back's name is Biakabatuka.

| | PLAY | YOUR NOTES |

Play 1

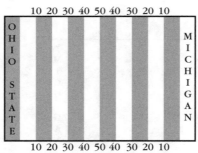

PLY

Play 2

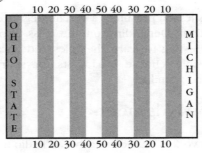

Play 3

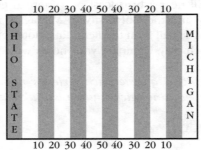

Play 4

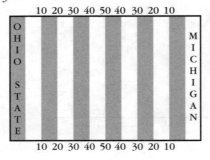

Appendix B: Broadcast Transcript

B. Check your comprehension, and practice retelling what is happening in the four plays with your partner.

Play 1

Broadcaster: And Biakabatuka is finally brought down at the fifty yard line. That'll be first down and ten for Michigan at the fifty yard line. Biakabatuka running with a calf injury . . . six rushes today for over sixty yards so far. So Michigan has the ball at mid-field, driving against the number two team in the country.

Play 2

Broadcaster: And off to Biakabatuka, up the middle, he breaks a tackle at the forty, another one at the thirty-five, to the thirty! He's in the clear, he goes down to the twenty! To the ten! And finally, brought down and run out of bounds at the seven yard line! Forty-three yards for Biakabatuka on the run up the middle! And Michigan has first and goal at the seven!

Play 3

Broadcaster: . . . He's down at the seven yard line. First and goal for Michigan, three nothing, Ohio State, midway through the first quarter, but Michigan is now threatening to score . . . at the Ohio State seven, ball on the left hash mark, Griese at quarterback. And off to Biaka-batuka, again up the middle and he's brought down at the four yard line! He falls forward for a three-yard gain. It will be second down and goal. Nice open field tackle by Number 13 for Ohio State . . . .

Play 4

Broadcaster: Man in motion, Biakabatuka in the backfield, the fake, the hand-off, Griese rolls out to his right, he looks into the end zone, finds a receiver, open, TOUCHDOWN! TOUCHDOWN, MICHIGAN! Number 33, four-yard touchdown from Griese! . . . Six to three, Michigan!

Contributor

Maricel G. Santos is an EFL instructor at the Language Center of Kwansei Gakuin University, Nishinomiya, Japan.

Part II: Newspapers, Magazines, and Literature

Editors' Note

This section explores some uses of printed news media. The overview demonstrates that there are not only many genres of writing available as input for students but also that a variety of skills can be practiced using the print media, from discussion, to essay organization, to grammar practice. This section is divided into three parts: News; Advice and Opinion; and Ads, Interviews, and Stories. The articles included here are just a sampling of what creative teachers might develop from the various news media.

◆ News Protest!

Levels
Intermediate +

Aims
Develop reading and
writing skills and
strategies

Class Time
45 minutes–1 hour

Preparation Time
20 minutes

Resources
Newspaper article
Work sheet

This lesson is an ideal way to get students to discuss and debate current controversial issues and learn and understand new vocabulary. The activity lends itself to any type of current issue that can be found in newspapers and magazines: race relations, death penalty, gun control, drugs, crime, environmental concerns.

Procedure

1. Locate an article of appropriate length on controversial issue, such as reproductive rights (see Appendix A).
2. Prepare vocabulary list and question work sheet (see Appendix B).
3. Assign article for homework or give students time in class to read and understand vocabulary.
4. Have students skim the article for the answers to questions on the work sheet.
5. Have students write one-paragraph summaries of the article.
6. Place students in small groups or pairs to share their answers and summaries.
7. As a whole class or in small groups, discuss the issue in the article. Compare U.S. attitudes on this issue to those in other countries.
8. Make lists on the board or on poster paper illustrating these ideas.

Caveats and Options

1. This type of reading and discussion can lead to a more formal debate type of activity. The instructor can choose student teams to represent the pro and con sides of the issue in the article and facilitate a formal argument. Each team should be given time to present their opinions and facts as well as to ask questions of the opposing team. The time allotment should be determined by the instructor. A good time limit

for debate is 30 minutes–1 hour, depending on proficiency levels. The audience can vote at the end of the discussion.

2. Students can also write essays that discuss their own personal views and opinions on controversial topics or write a compare-and-contrast essay regarding opinions in the United States and their own countries.

References and Further Reading

Connell, E. L., Lewis, M., Turner, J., Kling, J., & Tickle, A. (1995, March). *Building a content-based program: A dynamic dialogue*. Colloquium presented at the 29th Annual TESOL Convention, Long Beach, CA.

Connell, E. L., & Partch, P. (1995, January). *Reality bites: Adapting authentic materials into comprehensible chunks*. Workshop at Steinbeck Regional CATESOL Conference, Monterey, CA.

Hulse, M. L. (1994, March). *Developing a content course: A template*. Paper presented at the 28th Annual TESOL Convention, Baltimore, MD.

Appendix A: Sample Article

There are many articles of this format in local papers (from wire services like Associated Press) that intermediate- to advanced-level ESL students can easily comprehend. This particular article from Associated Press briefly covers the antiabortion protest on Capitol Hill on January 23, 1995. The article describes the march in nine easy-to-understand paragraphs. Some basic facts and the platform for antiabortion groups are explained.

Anti-abortion protesters march on Supreme Court

WASHINGTON (AP) — Thousands of anti-abortion protesters marched from the White House to the Supreme Court yesterday, chanting prayers, shouting slogans and waving white crosses in an annual protest against the 1973 Supreme Court decision legalizing abortion.

"Rejoice, rejoice — my mom was not pro-choice," many shouted as they walked along downtown Washington streets on a cloudy, chilly afternoon.

"Abortion is not and never will be respectable," march organizer Nellie Gray, president of March for Life Inc., said at an hourlong rally in a grassy park just south of the White House. "No one has the right to murder with impunity."

After an hour's walk to the Supreme Court, hundreds of people knelt on the court's steps to pray as police in riot gear looked on. A black-and-white poster of an aborted fetus was propped up nearby.

U.S. Park Police estimated the crowd at 45,000; Gray put the number at 100,000. Last year, about 35,000 people braved an ice storm to march against abortion.

Some demonstrators blocked traffic and later 39 protesters were arrested after blocking one of the doors of the Department of Health and Human Services building to demonstrate against fetal tissue research.

Activists on both sides of the issue were holding rallies, prayer vigils and demonstrations to mark the Supreme Court's 1973 Roe vs.

Wade ruling. The actual anniversary was Sunday.

Some at yesterday's march denounced recent shootings at abortion clinics. Four people were killed and six wounded at shootings at abortion clinics last year in the United States and Canada.

Clinic violence hurts the anti-abortion movement, said the Rev. Tom Pettei from St. Francis Prep School in Fresh Meadows, N.Y. "It mixes the message," he said. "This is a cause for life."

Monterey Peninsula Herald, January 24, 1995. Used with permission.
Copyright © *Monterey Peninsula Herald*.

Appendix B: Sample Work Sheet to Accompany Article

Anti-abortion protesters march on Supreme Court, *Monterey Peninsula Herald* (January 24, 1995)

1. Review this vocabulary:
   - *protesters*
   - *impunity*
   - *prayer vigils*
   - *fetus*
   - *propped up*
   - *chanting*
   - *rally*

2. Skim the article and answer the following questions:
   - Who?
   - What?
   - Where?
   - When?
   - Why?
   - How?

3. Summarize the article in your own words:

Contributor

Eve L. Connell is a public speaking and business English specialist and teacher trainer for the MA programs at the Monterey Institute of International Studies as well as an ESL instructor at Monterey Peninsula College, in California, in the United States.

Using Newspaper Captions as Writing Models

Levels
Beginning

Aims
Write well-punctuated, grammatical sentences
Make captions for photographs of field trips or other class activities

Class Time
15–60 minutes

Preparation Time
Time to take pictures and have them developed

Resources
Photographs of people, places, and things familiar to students
Newspaper photographs, with captions

In this activity, students write their own captions for pictures they have taken, using captions in newspapers as models. Because students are familiar with the people and places in the pictures, and they know that their classmates will be reading their captions, they are motivated to write interesting sentences. Also, because they are such short pieces of writing, they can easily be revised until they are perfect. The pictures and captions can be displayed on a bulletin board or in a student newspaper.

Procedure

1. Show newspaper photos with captions as examples (see Appendix A). Point out that captions describe an action or identify people and places, and that they are short, usually one or two sentences. Captions tell what is important about the photo and hint about the story.
2. Put several of the caption examples on the board or overhead. Point out subjects and verbs in each sentence as well as capital letters beginning and periods ending each sentence. Discuss verb tenses used. (Convention most often dictates simple present, but you will find examples of present progressive, simple past, and others.)
3. Give students several example newspaper photos with captions cut off and ask them to write a caption for each photo. Next, give out the real captions so that students can compare their caption with the original.
4. Distribute real photographs (see Appendix B) that were taken either by you during a recent field trip or school event or by the students themselves. Be sure that each student has at least one photo. Instruct students to write one caption for each picture.
5. Supervise peer checking of sentences in pairs for appropriateness, grammar, spelling, and punctuation. Ask students to rewrite their sentences correctly and neatly.

6. Display the captioned photos on the bulletin board or in a student newspaper. Black-and-white prints photocopy better than color photos.

Caveats and Options

1. Focus on particular language points students are studying. For example, students may want to distinguish between the simple present tense and present progressive tense.
2. If the pictures fall naturally into a logical sequence, you can have the students put them in order. You may want them to link the sentences, using conjunctions or other connectors.
3. This is a good way to begin to teach editing and revision. Sentences might have to be modified when they are combined (e.g., a repeated noun would be changed to a pronoun).
4. The groups of captions can be used as a dictation exercise.
5. The photos and captions can be used for a concentration game. Captions are written in large letters with markers on index cards. Face-down photos and captions are picked up as students attempt to make matches.

Appendix A: Sample Photograph and Caption

Southern Illinoisan photo by JOE JINES

Merchandise: Mae Batteau of 806 W. Cherry in Marion has a yard sale just about every week. The Marion City Council is considering putting a limit on how often residents have yard sales.

Appendix B: Sample Photograph and Caption Written by Student

Photo: Lynne Davis.
Used with permission.

This is Hideo Nomo. He is wearing a plaid shirt.

Contributor

Lynne Davis is general English coordinator at the Center for English as a Second Language, Southern Illinois University, in the United States.

Adverbials X

Levels
Intermediate +

Aims
Look at real-world
adverbial problems
Review specific
grammar points focusing
on meaning and
pragmatics
Analyze ambiguously
worded texts

Class Time
45 minutes

Preparation Time
20 minutes +

Resources
Newspaper article

A dverbials can create subtle problems of meaning and open up the door to unintended interpretation, sometimes humorous, other times costly. It is often ambiguous which part of a sentence an adverbial modifies and how broad the domain of modification reaches. This is particularly true when language is taken out of its intended context.

Procedure

1. Distribute article "Misleading Language on Driver's Licenses is Costly for Some Motorists" (see Appendix A) and have students read it. This particular text is ideal because of the problem caused by the two adverbials found in the driver's license legal wording. The placement in the problematic statement makes their respective domains of modification ambiguous:

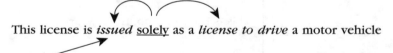

This license is *issued* solely as a *license to drive* a motor vehicle

in this state; it does not establish eligibility for employment, voter

registration, or public benefits.

2. In groups or pairs, have students answer questions related to the article (see Appendix B).
3. While the groups are working, give each group another example of fine print, doublespeak, or loopholes in official documents (see Lyneham, n.d.; Pei, 1973, for suggestions). Each group will examine

and analyze the new text when they have finished answering the questions above.

4. The groups will present their text to the entire class, explaining what to watch out for and how the language could be made clearer.

Caveats and Options

1. This activity might supplement some other playful examples and a discussion of syntax and word order when using adverbials.
2. Examples of doublespeak can be found in advertisements and other official documents.

References and Further Reading

Lyneham, P. (n.d.). *Politic speak: The bemused voters' guide to insults, promises, leadership coups, media grabs, pork-barreling and old-fashioned double-speak*. New York: ABC Enterprises.

Pei, M. A. (1973). *Double-speak in America*. New York: E. P. Dutton.

van Lier, L. (1995). *Introducing language awareness*. London: Penguin English.

Appendix A: Sample Article

Misleading language on driver's licenses is costly for some motorists

BY TED BELL

McClatchy News Service

SACRAMENTO — Nobody expected that the phrase "solely ... in this state" on driver's licenses would lead to the arrest and fining of California motorists by state troopers throughout the nation — at a cost to state taxpayers of almost $250,000.

But that is what has resulted from a bill designed to stop illegal immigrants from using easily obtained California driver's licenses to gain documents such as visas and work permits.

Under SB 946, sponsored by State Sen. Alfred Alquist, D-San Jose, all California driver's licenses issued after July 1 were printed to include the following notice:

"This license is issued solely as a license to drive a motor vehicle in this state; it does not establish eligibility for employment, voter registration, or public benefits."

The problems arose when some law enforcement agencies in other states interpreted the word "solely" to mean the licenses restrict the use of a motor vehicle to California only — instead of a license just for operating a motor vehicle, said Department of Motor Vehicles spokesman Bill Madison.

Madison said drivers, mostly truckers, have been shut down or fined for driving without a valid license in Indiana, Texas, Tennessee, West Virginia and Virginia.

"My drivers were being stopped at ports of entry and department of transportation checkpoints," said Riley Norton, vice president of P.S.T. Vans, whose Salt Lake City-based company hires California drivers. "I had 15 or 20 stopped, six within just a few days."

Norton wrote the California DMV and Gov. Wilson in late July, and that was the first the DMV heard about the problem, said Madison.

The state agency then began mailing letters to anyone who had received a new license or renewal since July. Each letter had a portion to be snipped off and kept with the license — with new language.

Appendix B: Group Activity Sheet

Directions: Read the article and answer the questions below.

1. What went wrong?
2. What was the source of the problem?
3. What were the consequences?
4. How would you try to explain the problem to a police officer if you were pulled over for a traffic violation in another state?

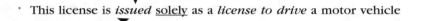

· This license is *issued* <u>solely</u> as a *license to drive* a motor vehicle

<u>in this state</u>; it does not establish eligibility for employment, voter

registration, or public benefits.

5. Is the license to be used only in this state? Or only to drive a motor vehicle? Both? Neither?
6. How could you change the wording to make it clearer?

Contributors

Jessica Buchsbaum teaches in San Francisco, California, in the United States. Robert Cole is an instructor at the Monterey Institute of International Studies, in the United States. Leigh Schleicher works for the Minnesota Department of Children, Families and Learning, in St. Paul, Minnesota, in the United States.

◆ Advice and Opinion Hearing Voices

Levels
High intermediate

Aims
Recognize the importance of sentence structure and vocabulary in establishing voice in written text

Class Time
45 minutes

Preparation Time
30 minutes

Resources
Letters to the editor from newspapers or news magazines

Students need to recognize how writers make their feelings known and their voices heard in their writings. This activity encourages students to read critically, be aware of their own voices in their writings, and experience an important pastime in U.S. culture: sounding off.

Procedure

1. Locate suitable letters to the editor from a newspaper or news magazine. The letters should demonstrate the different ways writers use sentence structure and vocabulary to show their feelings about a topic, such as:
    ● rhetorical questions: *Why is it that people such as council members make decisions on matters they have no clue about?*
    ● sarcasm: *I feel really safe in the parks now, with the policy that replaces park rangers with work release prisoners.*
    ● loaded vocabulary: *It is this kind of ludicrous thinking that has been used time and again to hoodwink voters.*
    ● expressions: *Alas!*
    ● italics or underlining: *The arts are some of the last bastions of civilization.*
    ● dialect grammar: *This ain't your kind of town.*
2. Pass out copies of the letters to the students. (See Appendix for sample.)
3. Choose one letter to analyze with the students. Using a transparency, identify the different techniques writers use to make their voices heard, their feelings known.
4. Pretend you are the writer and read the letter aloud, using intonation, stress, and gestures to convey the writer's feelings.
5. Pair the students and assign one letter to each pair.

6. Ask the pairs to analyze their letters for writing techniques that give information about the writer's feelings.
7. Ask the pairs to give voices to their writers by reading the letters aloud to the class, using the appropriate intonation, stress, and gestures.
8. Ask the pairs to support their choice of voices by reporting to the class what techniques the writers used.

Caveats and Options

1. As a variation, remove the names from the letters and have students guess whether the writers are women or men.
2. This reading-writing activity can be expanded into a longer conversation activity by discussing the contents of the letters, the likelihood of some of the letters appearing in newspapers in the students' countries, or the students' reactions to the voices behind some of the letters (e.g., those that seem threatening or insulting).
3. Ask the students to write a letter to the editor of the school newspaper, voicing their opinions on a controversial issue such as a proposed hike in parking fees. Encourage them to use the techniques studied in order to make their feelings known.
4. Ask the students to write a letter to the editor of the school newspaper, voicing their opinions on a controversial issue such as a proposed hike in parking fees. Encourage them to use the techniques studied to make their feelings known.

**Appendix:
Sample
Editorial,
With Student
Activity Sheet**

Editorial 'bites': Dumb, irresponsible

I've long thought of The Observer's editorials as bland, characterless, Styrofoam, weak and unopinionated, designed not to offend, and certainly incapable of changing a reader's opinion or directing new light on an important issue.

Now you are plumbing new depths with the recent addition of short editorial "bites." Inane remarks on such topics as "Baywatch" and beer bellies are pure sawdust filler. While these snippets are meant to be entertaining, they are sorely misplaced on an editorial page.

Not that outtakes, quotes or summaries from others' work cannot work well. Sunday's Observations column, one of The Observer's strongest features, makes a reader think, reflect and discuss.

Take seriously your responsibility as the only major regional newspaper. Stop dumbing down The Observer.

From *The Charlotte Observer.* Used with permission.

1. With your partner, read the letter to the editor. How does the writer describe the newspaper's editorials? Why do you think the writer chose those particular words and phrases?
2. Do you think the writer is advising or scolding the newspaper at the close of the letter? What helped you decide your answer?
3. Decide how the letter would sound if the writer were sitting with you, telling you her thoughts. Which words or phrases would the writer stress? What facial, hand, or body gestures would the writer use? What tone of voice would the writer use?
4. Read the letter aloud to your partner in the voice of the writer. Did you and your partner agree?
5. Decide on a voice with your partner and read the letter aloud to the class in the writer's voice. Explain your reasons for your choice. What techniques did the writer use that allowed you to hear her voice?

Contributor

Nancy Pfingstag is the writing coordinator for the English Language Training Institute of The University of North Carolina at Charlotte, in the United States.

"Dear Editor . . ." or Organizing an Opinion Essay

Levels
Intermediate +

Aims
Recognize standard
North American forms
of argumentation and
opinion writing

Class Time
50 minutes +

Preparation Time
15–30 minutes

Resources
Letters to the editor
from local and regional
newspapers and news
magazines

Students need to recognize standard approaches to developing a written argument. Letters to the editor are concise examples of argument structure found in longer essays and may be diagrammed easily without words, thus providing students with a clear picture of the structure behind what they are reading and how they can transfer that to their own writing.

Procedure

1. Ask students to choose a letter to the editor from samples you have chosen from the editorial page.
2. Ask each student to draw a diagram of the letter, using the following simple conventions:

   I = introduction (circle)
   C = conclusion (circle)
   i, ii, iii, etc. = a point raised in the argument, an example (box)
   (see Appendices A and B for examples)

3. Ask students to compare their diagrams and discuss any discrepancies.
4. Have students repeat Steps 2 and 3 at least once, possibly twice. Students have now diagrammed two or three letters to the editor.
5. Ask students to compare the two or three letters they have diagrammed, looking for similarities and differences.

Caveats and Options

1. Ask students to diagram a short article using the same conventions. Then ask them to compare their diagrams of letters to the editor with their diagrams of articles.
2. Ask students to use the structure of a letter (preferably one they have diagrammed themselves) to write their own letter to the editor, closely following the prescribed structure.
3. Students (and instructors) may wish to develop their own method of diagramming, perhaps introducing further symbols for different aspects of writing (e.g., diamonds to illustrate examples, an *L* to denote a list).
4. Students will also benefit from diagramming their written work or, if peer editing, the writing of their classmates, in order to make the structure of the writing clear.
5. Students may also like to make explicit the phrases that connect the various sections of their diagrams (e.g., with connecting words: *but, however, and on the other hand,* and others).

Acknowledgment

This lesson was developed in coordination with a graduate writing course taught by Cherry Campbell, at the Monterey Institute of International Studies. Campbell is now at Sonoma State University, in California, in the United States.

Appendix A: Sample Letter to the Editor 1

Stave Church in wrong location?

Guy Paulson's plan for a Norwegian stave church sounds like a wonderful gift for Moorhead. We appreciate the expense and effort he is giving.

However, I just can't help but wonder what might have been if the Heritage-Hjemkomst Interpretive Center, and now the stave church, had their home in a location next to I-94 rather than so well hidden down by the river. Just think of the tourists that would be compelled to stop after seeing such unusual buildings . . . and the tourist money that would be generated, and the support businesses that might have sprung up near it . . . and the tax dollars generated.

Oh well, just another example of tax dollars spent without location, location, location, in mind.

Nancy Otto
Moorhead

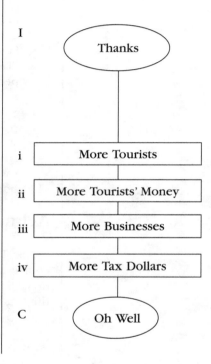

I — Thanks

i — More Tourists

ii — More Tourists' Money

iii — More Businesses

iv — More Tax Dollars

C — Oh Well

Reprinted with permission of *The Forum of Fargo, North Dakota,*

Appendix B: Sample Letter to the Editor 2

Students had excellent experience at Fargo's Washington High School

As our daughter completes sixth grade at Washington Elementary in Fargo, we are excited, sad and grateful. Our son began our relationship with Washington 10 years ago and it has been a wonderful experience every year.

We are excited to see them move on to new schools and new challenges. We are sad in that we will no longer have the opportunity to witness our children participate in band, choir and orchestra concerts, and other activities held at Washington.

We would like to take this opportunity to express our gratitude and thanks to the wonderful teachers and staff at Washington. Our job as parents has been much easier because of the caring attitudes and high standards of education they exhibit.

Our sincere thanks for all you have done for Justine and Natalie. A special thank you to Ron Thorson and Ron Messelt, your leadership has garnered your staff a report card with straight A's. We are forever grateful.

Pat and Patti Schmaltz
Fargo

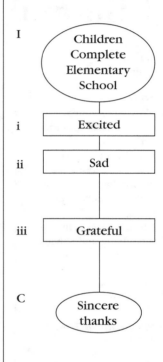

Reprinted with permission of *The Forum of Fargo, North Dakota*, and Pat and Patti Schmaltz.

Contributor

Paul Magnuson is a doctoral candidate in curriculum and instruction at the University of Minnesota and Dean of the English Language Village at Concordia Language Villages, in Moorhead, Minnesota, in the United States.

What Do You Think I Should Do?

Levels
Intermediate

Aims
Illustrate grammar
structures such as modal
verbs
Use the imperative
Monitor reading
comprehension of short
authentic newspaper
passages
Discuss approaches to
identifying and solving
problems

Class Time
2-3 hours

Preparation Time
1-2 hours

Resources
Advice columns from
newspapers and
magazines
Grammar reference for
modal verbs and
imperatives

D iscovering what a target culture perceives as problematic and how it goes about solving problems provides students with invaluable cultural insight. By using the authentic model of advice letters and responses, students can also learn how imperatives and modal verbs of advice, suggestion, and obligation are used in authentic written discourse.

Procedure

1. Review a few examples of how modal verbs can be used when giving advice, making suggestions, and expressing obligation. Also, review how the imperative can be used when giving advice.
2. Give each student a copy of a letter written to an advice column (e.g., "Dear Abbey" or "Ann Landers"). Each student should have a different one (see Appendix A).
3. Ask the students to read their letters and write a response to the person who has written it.
4. Give the students the copy of the original response to their letters written by the advice columnist.
5. Ask students to find similarities and differences between the advice they gave and the advice of the columnist and report their findings to the rest of the class. Students then discuss and draw conclusions, if they can, about the types of problems presented and advice offered in advice columns in the target language and culture. (See Appendix B for activity sheet.)
6. Next, students do self- and peer-correction of the modal verbs and imperatives used in each others' response letters.
7. Have students focus on the way the advice columnist gave advice. Did they use modal verbs? Did they use imperatives? Which verbs did

they use? If they didn't use modals or imperatives, how did they give the advice?

Caveats and Options

1. Students can work individually on the same letter. In this way the cultural differences among students can be discussed as well.
2. Students can be asked to work on one letter in a small group. They will need to come to some agreement in order to write a response. Have students report back to the class how they came to an agreement and what they discovered about their own individual differences.
3. Students can also be asked to write a response according to how someone of their parents' generation might respond. In this way, cultural changes between generations can also be discussed.
4. Write your own advice letters with accompanying responses based on problems that are very relevant to your students (e.g., dealing with a difficult roommate, feeling pressure to sleep with someone, being shy about expressing an opinion). In this way you can be certain that specific cultural points and issues will come up.
5. Have students bring in letters and responses that interest them from local papers. Have them comment on the advice-givers' use of language as well as the usefulness of their advice.
6. It should be made clear that there is no one right answer to each letter and that within and among all cultures there could be a variety of responses.
7. It may be intrusive to ask students to write their own "problem letters" as it may seem a bit too personal. Sometimes it is easier to deal with problems in the classroom that are depersonalized.
8. Have information handy on community resources and services in your area for students to refer to when writing response letters.

Appendix A: Sample Letter and Response

This is a sample of a letter and response from the "Ask Ange" column in the *Hong Kong Sunday Morning Post* (1996, June 2). It could be used with secondary-school-aged students.

> **Q:**   I have a mega crush on a girl but there is a slight problem. I don't know if she likes me or not. How do I find out if a girl likes me? I am too shy to ask her, and barely see her.
>
> **Curious, Hong Kong**
>
> **A:**   Stop wondering if she likes you and do something about it! Next time you see her introduce yourself and start a conversation. I realize that this is easier said than done when you are shy, but I promise that you will feel so much better about yourself if you gather up the courage and initiate a conversation with her. The first conversation will be the hardest, but once you have broken the ice, it will be easier to talk to her next time. So be brave and bold: talk to her and take things from there.

Used with permission. Copyright © *Hong Kong Sunday Morning Post.*

Appendix B: Student Activity Sheet

1. In your own words, describe the problem the writer has.
2. What do you think the writer should do?
3. Write an advice letter to the writer on the back of this handout.
4. Read the original advice columnist's response and then compare your advice to hers.
   How was it similar? How was it different?
5. What kind of language did the advice columnist use to give the advice (e.g., modals, imperatives)? What kind of language did you use?

Contributor

Maida Kennedy Xiao, a lecturer at Hong Kong Polytechnic University and a coauthor of two ESL texts on using film, has taught for 13 years.

◆ Ads, Interviews, and Stories
I'll Buy It!

Levels
Intermediate

Aims
Cooperate with group
members to reach
assigned goal
Make greater use of
negotiation strategies

Class Time
1 hour +

Preparation Time
45 minutes

Resources
Magazine
advertisements that
exemplify the use of
ethos, pathos, and logos

We have all been influenced by advertising to buy or not to buy, to do or not to do. Often we do not stop to think about these advertisements and why it is that they compel us to take some action. This activity is designed to make learners more aware of how advertising works and to provide an interesting topic for discussion by looking at three different types of advertising. Advertisements that use ethos (the appeal to one's sense of right and wrong) as a primary means of persuasion are the hardest to find, but some examples would be advertisements on saving the rain forest or the use of animals in drug testing. Pathos (the appeal to one's emotions, e.g., pride or sadness) is very common in advertisements. This type of advertisement is used to sell things like cars or the latest clothing and imply that a person can resemble the people depicted in the scene if he purchases the items. The use of logos (the use of logic or reason) is also fairly common and can be found in advertisements that list reasons to do something or compare things.

Persuasion can be used in positive and negative ways. The use of negative ideas or images can also be found in advertisements such as those for antismoking or political messages. These advertisements can also exemplify the use of ethos, pathos, and logos. Advertisements that use negativism try to present something in a negative light so that you will not want to use, buy, listen to, or support the item in the advertisement.

Procedure

1. Locate three types of advertisements (see Appendices A–C).
2. Divide the class into groups of three. These will be the home groups. If the class does not divide evenly into three, it is okay to have a few groups of four.
3. Explain to the students that they are going to do a cooperative jigsaw task and that they will learn some information to teach to the other members of their home groups.

4. Have the students number off and regroup into groups of like numbers (i.e., as Group 1, Group 2, and so on). These are the Study Groups.

5. Explain that the purpose of the Study Groups is to work together and help each other learn the material. Emphasize that all the members in the Study Group need to fully understand in order to explain their information to their Home Group members.

6. Distribute the group study sheets (see Appendix D) with inserted blurbs (see Appendix E) and corresponding advertisements (see Appendices A–C) to each of the three groups.

7. Tell the students to look at their advertisement and work together to answer the questions on the study sheet.

8. When the students in each of the groups have completed their study sheets, have them return to their home groups.

9. Tell them to complete the Home Group Study Questions (see Appendix F) but make sure they understand that they are not to show nor read from their previous work sheet to their home group members. They must tell their home group member about anything they learned in the previous group in their own words.

10. When the groups have finished, go over the home group questions together as a class. Encourage the students to express their ideas and opinions whenever possible.

Caveats and Options

1. If the teacher has access to a language lab where videos or play tapes can be shown, preferably three at once, one alternative would be to use TV or radio commercials. This would be especially good for more advanced classes or as a follow up to this lesson on written advertisements.

2. During the class discussion at the end of the task, one way to reinforce the concept of cooperation is to allow only one person in each home group to answer. The answer should be different for each question. The group gets a point if the person is correct but no point if the answer is wrong. The students will therefore want to be sure everyone can answer all of the questions so their group will get the most points. If you use this option, you should explain this to the students before the task.

References and Further Reading

Johnson, D. W., & Johnson, R. (1994). Cooperative learning in second language classes. *The Language Teacher, 18,* 4–7.

Johnson, D. W., & Johnson, R., & Holubec, E. (1993). *Circles of learning: Cooperation in the classroom* (3rd ed.). Edina, MN: Interaction Book Company.

Krashen, S. (1981). *Second language acquisition and second language learning.* London: Pergamon.

Long, M. (1983). Native speaker/non-native speaker conversation and the negotiation of comprehensible input. *Applied Linguistics, 4,* 126–141.

Pica, T. (1987). Second language acquisition, social interaction, and the classroom. *Applied Linguistics, 8,* 3–21.

Swain, M. (1986). Communicative competence: Some roles of comprehensive input and comprehensible output in its development. In S. Gass & C. Madden (Eds.), *Input in second language acquisition.* Rowley, MA: Newbury House.

Appendix A: Magazine Advertisement— Ethos

WHEN IT'S YOUR

COMPANY,

YOU GO TO THE ENDS OF THE

EARTH

TO MAKE IT WORK.

OVER 500 DESTINATIONS ACROSS 6 CONTINENTS.

To some, it is merely a noble sentiment. But to us, "going to the ends of the earth" is a mandate.

That's why we offer over 500 destinations across 6 continents. And we'll be adding new destinations like Malaysia, the Philippines and Frankfurt from Eastern Canada. We are also the #1 Canadian carrier to Asia with over 35 flights, weekly. In fact, when you consider our alliance with American Airlines,* Lufthansa, Qantas, Varig, Mandarin Airlines, Alitalia* and Air New Zealand—the ends of the Earth are truly at your doorstep. Indeed, we're going further. Why? Because when your company depends on the satisfaction of your customers, anything less just wouldn't fly. Call us at 1-800-665-1177, or visit our web site at http://www.cdnair.ca

Canadi⧫n

✈ GOING FURTHER

 Canadian is a registered trademark of Canadian Airlines International Ltd.
American Airlines is a registered trademark of American Airlines, Inc. *As of November 1, 1995.

Used with permission of Canadian Airlines.

**Appendix B:
Magazine
Advertisement—
Pathos**

A Monarch Butterfly
can migrate from
the Great Lakes
to the mountains
of Mexico
and back again,
often drifting from
its predetermined
course, but never, ever
losing its way.

Now, which way
is that trail?

With the new Magellan GPS 2000, you can find your way back to any
landmark, destination or campsite, anytime. The hand-held GPS 2000
uses satellite navigation technology to instantly pinpoint where you are,
where you've been, and where you're going. It's rugged, waterproof,
compact, and surprisingly affordable. It's also push-button easy. How easy
is that? Try pushing these buttons for
more information and the dealer nearest
you: 1-800-707-7841. Try it now.

MAGELLAN
WE BRING GPS DOWN TO EARTH.™

Magellan Systems Corporation, 960 Overland Ct., San Dimas, CA 91773 Phone: (909) 394-5000 Fax: (909) 394-7050

CIRCLE NO. 135 ON READER SERVICE CARD

Used with permission
of Magellan Systems
Corporation.

Appendix C: Magazine Advertisement— Logos

Appendix D: Group Study Sheet

Directions: In your group discuss the following questions. Make sure everyone understands the answers.

1. Look at your advertisement. What is it trying to get you to do? Buy something? Change your mind? Do something?
2. Explain why you feel that the advertisement is trying to do this.
3. Is this advertisement positive or negative? Why do you think so?
4. How is the advertisement trying to persuade you? Is it trying to reason with you, appeal to your emotions, or appeal to your feelings of right and wrong?
5. How does the advertisement try to appeal to you in this way?
6. Why do you think the advertisers are trying to appeal to you in this way?
7. Is this advertisement effective? Why or why not?
8. Where (or in which type of publication) would you expect to see this kind of advertisement?

   [The teacher should insert either the ethos, pathos, or logos paragraphs from Appendix E here.]

9. Think of some more examples of advertisements using this type of persuasion you have seen.

Appendix E: Group Study Sheet Inserts

Study Sheet: Group 1—Ethos

One way of persuading people to do something is to appeal to their sense of right and wrong. This type of persuasion is sometimes used in advertising like the one you are looking at. Its purpose is to motivate people to act because they feel that something is morally incorrect.

Study Sheet: Group 2—Logos

One way of persuading people to change their way of thinking is by reasoning logically with them. This type of persuasion is very common in advertising. The advertisement your group is looking at is an example of this type of advertising.

Appendix F: Home Group Study Questions

Study Sheet: Group 3—Pathos

One way to persuade a person to change their way of thinking is to appeal to their emotions. This form of persuasion is very common in advertising. Advertisers often try to make us feel happy, sad, nostalgic, etc. in their advertisements. The advertisement you are looking at is an example of this type of advertising.

Directions: Discuss the following questions in your group. Make sure everyone in your group understands the questions and has the correct answer.

1. What are the different ways of persuasion?
2. Which form of persuasion do you think is most often used? Why?
3. What type of persuasion is most often used with negative ideas?
4. Which form of persuasion do you think would be best for the following advertisements:
   ● to get someone to buy an economy car; why?
   ● not to drink and drive; why?
   ● to visit the zoo; why?
   Do you think TV, radio, and print media use the same amount of negative advertising? If no, which one uses it the most? Which the least? Why?

In your group, write a 30-second radio advertisement. What form of persuasion will you use? Will it be negative or positive? Why did you make the choices you did?

Contributor

Spencer D. Weatherly is an EFL teacher at several universities in Tokyo, Japan. His interests include materials development, cooperative strategies in the EFL classroom, and language testing.

Interviewing a Star

Levels
Intermediate

Aims
Learn basic types of
questions needed to
make an interesting
report on a celebrity
Practice asking and
answering questions
Learn how to conduct
an interview and form
personal questions and
responses

Class Time
1–2 hours

Preparation Time
15 minutes

Resources
Copies of an interview
column from a
newspaper
Chalkboard or overhead
projector
Two copies of work
sheet

The simple format of an interview column from a newspaper or news magazine is particularly suitable for the ESL classroom. The questions are in the form of incomplete sentences that are completed by the interviewee. The answers are short sentences or phrases rich in adjectives and filled with personal data, all of which makes for involved and interesting reading. Because the column is written in casual language, it approximates speech and can be used as a springboard for oral interviews and dialogues among students.

Procedure

1. Go over the interview(s) with the class (see samples in Appendix A). Have several students rephrase the interviewer's incomplete sentences as complete questions, and the interviewee's replies as complete sentences. This can be done as an oral exercise or as a written exercise on the chalkboard.
2. Discuss unknown words and phrases used in the article.
3. Inquire about other questions that could be included in such an interview. List them on the board or on an overhead. Remind students that in the United States there are questions that people do not like to answer, such as those concerning age, money, and sex.
4. Have students write their own responses to the interview questions. (Use a copy of work sheet in Appendix B).
5. Get pairs of students to interview each other, filling in the blank form. (Use another copy of work sheet in Appendix B.)
6. Ask each partner to introduce the other to the class, referring to the complete interview form. This will involve the students in combining questions and answers in more complicated sentences.

Caveats and Options

1. Give a different article to each student. In groups, they can discuss the different answers they find to the same questions.
2. Have students compose their own interview forms and, using magazines as references, conduct an imaginary interview with a famous person in the news.

Appendix A: Sample Interviews

Chicago Tribune Magazine
FAST TRACK
By Cheryl Lavin

Sarah Chalke

Birthday: Aug. 27, 1976.

Birthplace: I was born in Ottawa [Ontario, Canada] and I moved to Vancouver [British Columbia] when I was 2.

Occupation: Actress.

Current home: Vancouver and Los Angeles.

Marital status: Single.

Working on: I play Becky on "Roseanne."

The last good movie I saw: "Legends of the Fall."

I stay home to watch: Every week my friends and I get together to watch "Melrose Place."

The book I've been reading: "The Chamber" by John Grisham.

Prized possession: My pictures. I take them all the time. I have 8-by-10 blow-ups all over my room and I have four huge albums.

Personal heroes: Steve Martin and Jodie Foster.

If I could do it over I'd: Have stronger vocal cords. I lose my voice all the time. It's very frustrating.

The one thing I can't stand: Watching the way our environment is going downhill, even though more and more people are making efforts to try and save it. At first I didn't notice the difference between the air in Los Angeles and Vancouver, but now I run in both places and [in L.A.] I can really feel it in my lungs. It's scary.

The best time of my life: Now. In September I'm starting at the University of British Columbia, but right now I'm having so much fun, not going to school and just spending time with my family and friends.

The worst time of my life: Grade 11, when I was working and going to school. My grandmother died that year and I was starting work and I wasn't allowed to come back for the funeral.

Most humbling experience: When I was little, my family was in Mexico and we visited an orphanage. There were hundreds of children there who didn't have anything, but they were happy and they worked together to survive. It made me never want to see any materialism again.

If I wasn't an actress, I'd be: Preparing for a law career.

Three words that best describe me: Happy, dedicated and energetic.

Chicago Tribune Magazine
FAST TRACK
By Cheryl Lavin

Jeremy Piven

Birthday: July 26, 1965.

Birthplace: I was born in Manhattan and grew up in Evanston.

Occupation: Actor.

Current home: Los Angeles.

Marital status: Single.

Car: A 1969 black Ford Bronco.

Working on: I'm on "Ellen" on ABC-TV; I'm in a movie, "Larger Than Life," with Bill Murray; and I star in the Chicago Theatres on the Air production of "Born Guilty," which airs at 8 p.m. today on WFMT-FM (98.7) radio.

Favorite pigout food: Sushi.

Nickname: Fresh.

Prized possession: A drum kit. I had one in junior high and my sister borrowed it and lost it. I still don't know how you can lose a drum set. Success meant being able to buy a new one.

Personal heroes: Walter Payton, Marlon Brando.

I've never been able to: Play for the Chicago Bears.

If I could do it over I'd: Redo every performance. That's just a freaky actor thing.

I'd give anything to meet: Nelson Mandela.

My fantasy is: I'm ripping down a rebound with Dennis Rodman.

The best advice my mother ever gave me: "Endings are important so don't leave things unfinished."

The one thing I can't stand: People who live in fear and are too afraid to take a chance.

People who knew me in high school thought I was: Strange. I ran with so many different crowds—football players, actors.

The best time of my life: It's coming up.

The worst time of my life: It hasn't happened yet.

If I wasn't an actor, I'd be: Banging on things, trying to get attention.

If I've learned one thing in life it's: Don't keeping falling into the same old patterns.

Major accomplishment: I directed a play, something I had never done before, and stuck with it.

Three words that best describe me: Gets the joke.

Chicago Tribune Magazine
FAST TRACK
By Cheryl Lavin

Susan Powter

Birthday: Dec. 22, 1957.

Birthplace: Sydney, Australia.

Occupation: Woman.

Current home: Los Angeles.

Marital status: Single.

Children: Two sons, 13 and 12, and we're adopting a little girl.

Car: A green BMW. I don't know what year or model it is, but it has lots of numbers on it.

Working on: A new cookbook, "C'mon America, Let's Eat!" and two videos—lots of projects to help women get well.

The last good movie I saw: "Miracle on 34th Street."

The book I've been reading: "Permanent Midnight" (Warner Books), by Jerry Stahl.

Favorite pigout food: I eat too much every day, but not too much fat. If it's salty or spicy, count me in.

Favorite childhood memory: I don't have any.

Prized possession: Photographs of my children.

Personal heroes: Susan B. Anthony and Eleanor Roosevelt and all the other women who made it possible for women today to live the lives we're living.

Nobody knows I'm: Quiet, private.

I wish I could stop: I want to continue everything, even the mistakes, because I'm learning from them.

I've never been able to: Draw.

If I could do it over I: Would have understood, at an earlier age, that we're all given the ability to do anything we want.

I'd give anything to meet: Susan B. Anthony, and I intend to in the next life.

My fantasy is: I have long, thick, big hair. I'd pay $10,000 for Cindy Crawford's hair.

My most irrational act: Self-destruction.

My friends like me because: I'm as honest as I can possibly be in the moment.

Major accomplishment: My family. It's functional and wonderful.

Most humbling experience: Weighing 268 pounds, being unhealthy and unhappy and unable to function—so disconnected from me I didn't know who "me" was.

The words that best describe me: Tireless, committed and rough around the edges

Appendix B: Sample Interview Form

Name: _____ Birthday:_____

Birthplace: _____

Current Home (Address): _____

Occupation: _____ Marital Status: _____

The last good movie I saw: _____

Favorite performers (actors/musicians): _____

Prized possession (favorite thing): _____

Personal heroes: _____

I wish I could stop: _____

The worst advice my mother ever gave me: _____

My friends like me because: _____

I'd give anything to have met (I wish I had met): _____

I hope I never have to: _____

My fantasy is: _____

Three words that best describe me: _____

Additional questions:

Contributors

Constance Kappas is currently instructor of ESL at Black Hawk College, in Moline, Illinois. Marit Vamarasi is associate professor of linguistics at Northeastern Illinois University, in Chicago, Illinois, in the United States.

TV Time

Levels
Intermediate

Aims
Describe a culture based
on the content of its
media
Read a timetable
Discuss likes and
dislikes

Class Time
2 hours

Preparation Time
20–30 minutes

Resources
Television programming
schedule

Television networks and programs are created to appeal to different segments of a culture. Some networks, like ESPN, appeal to people interested in sports. Others, like Cable News Network, provide for those wanting access to news at any time. Some programs are designed to appeal to a female audience, some to a male audience; some programs are designed for children, some for adults.

Procedure

1. Make a copy of the television schedule grid from the newspaper for one day's programming.
2. Ask students their opinion of television. You may want to ask them to complete a work sheet to stimulate their thoughts (see Appendix A).
3. Have students break into small groups. Pass out one copy of the TV grid (see sample in Appendix B) to each group.
4. Ask groups to examine the grid, focusing on any four networks of their choice.
5. Ask groups to look at the program titles and descriptions (if given) for each of these networks.
6. Ask groups to write a description, based on these titles and descriptions, of the typical viewer of each of their selected networks. What would be the age and gender of the viewer? What personality traits would the viewer display? What level of education and what occupation would the viewer have?
7. Ask groups to discuss what the existence of the various networks reveals about the target culture.
8. Ask students, as a class, to share their group findings.

9. Ask students to think about the types of television networks and programs that exist in their native cultures and the typical viewer of each of these networks.

10. Ask students to individually compose a written comparison of television in their target culture and in their native culture. Have students include their views on how well the television programming reflects the values of the culture in which it is viewed.

Caveats and Options

1. Step 2 is a schema builder for students familiar with television. If you have students who are not, adapt this schema builder to their needs.

2. Students may work individually on Step 10 or in groups made up of students who share a native culture.

3. Students may bring in television schedules of programming in their native cultures to share with the class.

4. If students come from areas where television viewing is not common, end with Step 9.

References and Further Reading

Chan, D., Kaplan-Weinger, J., & Sandstrom, D. (1995). *Journeys to cultural understanding*. Boston: Heinle & Heinle.

Appendix A: Student Activity Sheet

Directions: Answer the following questions and be prepared to discuss them in class.

1. My favorite television program in my culture is:

2. I like this program because:

3. The best thing about television is:

4. The worst thing about television is:

5. Many people own televisions because:

6. Some programs are not appropriate for young children because:

7. One difference between television in my native culture and television in my target culture is:

8. The positive effects that television has on society are:

9. The negative effects that television has on society are:

Appendix B: Sample Television Grid

Friday, June 21, 1996

Friday night/6 p.m.-3 a.m.

© indicates closed-captioned programming.

Reprinted with permission of Tribune Media Services.

Contributors

Judith Kaplan-Weinger, Deborah Sandstrom, and Debra Chan are university educators in linguistics and TESL at Northwestern Illinois University and University of Illinois at Chicago, in the United States.

What an Adventure!

Levels
Advanced

Aims
Think about the environment and be able to discuss it
Make use of higher level reading skills such as inferencing and predicting

Class Time
1 hour +

Preparation Time
1 hour

Resources
Story or article on the environment

The condition of the environment has become a concern for scientists and others. For some people though, the environment is not important. This lack of concern can be due to many things but perhaps one of the most common reasons is a person's perceived proximity to the wilderness. People who live most or all of their lives in cities often do not realize just how close they live to the wilderness much less the interesting things there are to do and see there.

Procedure

1. Divide the class into groups of four. These will be the home groups. If the class does not divide evenly into four, it is okay to have a few groups of five.
2. Explain to the students that they are going to do a cooperative jigsaw task and that they will learn some information that they will teach to the other members of their home groups.
3. Have the students number off in each group.
4. Have the students regroup into groups of like numbers: all of the 1s together, 2s together, etc. These are the study groups.
5. Explain the purpose of the study groups: to work together and help each other learn the material. Emphasize that all the members in the study group need to fully understand in order to be able to explain their information to their home group members.
6. Distribute the study sheets to each of the four groups (see Appendices A–D).
7. Tell the students to work together and discuss the questions at the top of the page.
8. Go over the questions after the students have had time to talk about them. Encourage the students to volunteer their opinions.

9. Have the students read their part of the story and discuss the questions at the end.

10. When the students in all of the groups have completed discussing the questions that follow the reading, have them return to their home groups.

11. Tell them to complete the Home Group Discussion Questions (see Appendix E), but make sure they understand that they are not to show nor read from their previous work sheet to their home group members. They must tell their home group members about their part of the story and anything they learned in the previous group in their own words.

12. When the groups have finished, go over the Home Group work sheet together as a class. Encourage the students to express their ideas and opinions whenever possible.

Caveats and Options

1. For intermediate classes the teacher might prepare a vocabulary work sheet that the students could work on in class before they do the jigsaw task.

2. During the class discussion at the end of the task, one way to reinforce the concept of cooperation is to allow only one person in each home group to answer. A different person should answer each question. The group gets a point if the person is correct but no point if the answer is wrong. The students will therefore want to be sure everyone can answer all of the questions so their group will get the most points.

3. Another way to ensure cooperation would be to give the students a quiz (see Appendix F) before going over the home group discussion questions. Explain to the students that they will all get the same grade on the quiz because you will average their scores. Therefore, it is important to learn the materials so that everyone will get a high score.

References and Further Reading

Coelho, E. (1991). *Jigsaw.* Markham, Canada: Pippin.

Johnson, D. W., & Johnson, R. (1994). *Cooperative learning in second language classes. The Language Teacher, 18,* 4–7.

Johnson, D. W., Johnson, R., & Holubec, E. (1993). *Circles of learning: Cooperation in the classroom* (3rd ed.). Edina, MN: Interaction Book Company.

Shlomo, S. (Ed.). (1994). *Handbook of cooperative learning methods.* Westport, CT: Greenwood Press.

Slavin, R. (1990). *Cooperative learning.* Englewood Cliffs, NJ: Prentice Hall.

Acknowledgments

All of the excerpts in Appendices A–D are from "The Schmo of Kilimanjaro," D. Pinkwater, in *Fish Whistle,* © 1989 Daniel Pinkwater. Reprinted by permission of Addison-Wesley Publishing Company, Inc.

Appendix A: Study Group 1

Directions: In your groups discuss the following questions:

- Have you ever been in the wilderness? Where? When? What did you see there?
- If you have never been, would you like to go sometime?
- Where would you like to go?
- What would you expect to see in the wilderness?
- Do you think it is possible to live one's whole life and never see the wilderness? Why or why not?
- What do you think the title means?

The Schmo of Kilimanjaro

My friend Ken Kelman is a genius—a playwright and film critic. He's lived his whole life in Manhattan, and, I believe, until he was a grown adult, never had an unobstructed view of the sky. Certainly, outside of the zoo, he'd never seen anything of the natural world. What he did, mainly, was sit in dark theaters.

For some reason—I still don't know why—he agreed to take a trip to Africa with me. I explained to Kelman that something we'd be doing a lot of on our trip would be going around in a wilderness, spotting animals.

"That's OK by me," Kelman said. He was ready to have a good time. Given that Kelman had never been out of doors except to go from one building in Manhattan to another, I thought I might give him a sort of crash course in wildlife watching.

- Why do you think Kelman decided to take the trip to Africa?
- How do you think the crash course in wildlife watching went?
- Where do you think they went for this course?
- Do you think Kelman still wanted to go to Africa?
- What would you like to know about Kelman and his friend (the author)? Write down at least five questions that you have about the story.

Appendix B: Study Group 2

Directions: In your groups discuss the following questions:

- Have you ever been in the wilderness? Where? When? What did you see there?
- If you have never been, would you like to go sometime? Where would you like to go?
- What would you expect to see in the wilderness?
- Do you think it is possible to live one's whole life and never see the wilderness? Why or why not?
- What do you think the title means?

The Schmo of Kilimanjaro

A good thing about New York City is the proximity of large state parks and rural areas. If you don't live there, this might never occur to you. Within an hour or two of midtown, I have seen eagles, foxes, flights of geese, beaver dams, and have walked miles of forest trails.

I decided to take Kelman along a stretch of the Appalachian Trail, and point a few things out to him. He liked the idea. We drove about an hour and a half up the Taconic Parkway, and started walking. It was a good day for fauna. It was like a Disney nature film. Every few yards there was some woodland creature or other. Kelman missed them all.

"Look! a red-tailed hawk!"

"Where? Where?" The hawk waited as long as it could—but Kelman never focused on it.

"Shh! Look! Deer!"

"Deer? Where!"

- Do you think Kelman had been on the Appalachian trail before? Why do you think they went there?
- Why do you think Kelman missed the animals?
- Do you think Kelman had a good time?
- What would you like to know about Kelman and his friend (the author)? Write down at least five questions that you have about the story.

Appendix C: Study Group 3

Directions: In your groups discuss the following questions:

- Have you ever been in the wilderness? Where? When? What did you see there?
- If you have never been, would you like to go sometime? Where would you like to go?
- What would you expect to see in the wilderness?
- Do you think it is possible to live one's whole life and never see the wilderness? Why or why not?
- What do you think the title means?

The Schmo of Kilimanjaro

I decided to concentrate on one species. Chipmunks. There were chipmunks by the thousands, romping around in the underbrush. As we walked, I tried to point one out to my friend. Never did he lay eyes on one. At times it was hard to progress without squashing one—but did he see one? He did not.

I was exasperated.

On the way back to the car, there, sitting on a stump was a chipmunk—a fat, insolent one.

It didn't move.

Kelman noticed it.

He stared at it.

"That's a chipmunk?" Kelman asked.

"That is a chipmunk."

He looked some more. "Close to a cat," he said.

- Why do you think they were concentrating on chipmunks?
- Why do you think Kelman never saw a chipmunk while they were walking?
- Do you think chipmunks look like cats?
- Do you think Kelman had fun?
- What would you like to know about Kelman and his friend (the author)? Write down at least five questions that you have about the story.

Appendix D: Study Group 4

Directions: In your groups discuss the following questions:

- Have you ever been in the wilderness?
- Where? When? What did you see there?
- If you have never been, would you like to go sometime?
- Where would you like to go?
- What would you expect to see in the wilderness?
- Do you think it is possible to live one's whole life and never see the wilderness? Why or why not?
- What do you think the title means?

The Schmo of Kilimanjaro

So we flew to Africa. He wasn't on the ground for two hours before a large animal had its claws on him. We'd dropped off our bags at Brunner's Hotel, and gone straight out to the animal orphanage at the Nairobi Game Park. This is a sort of zoo where foundlings and wild pets that have grown up are kept. The management encourages many of the inmates to go over the wall, and live free in the game preserve.

There were a bunch of bears, confiscated from an Indian circus for abuse. Kelman leaned up against the stock-wire enclosure to take a picture, and one of the bears grabbed him by the jacket.

"Hey! Cut it out!" Kelman giggled.

I dragged Kelman away from the bear. The bear had a good hold on him.

"Quit horsing around!" Kelman said to me. "I'm trying to take a picture."

"That bear was trying to drag you through the fence!" I said.

"Sure. That's what I would do if I were a bear," Kelman said.

Later, when we were actually on safari, he told me one morning that he wanted to find someone to complain to. He was mad. It seems a big yellow dog had been running around outside the tent making noise in the night. It woke Kelman up and he finally had gone out and chased it away.

"People should tie up their dogs at night."

I went out, and sure enough, there were some good footprints, about nine inches across.

"Kelman, that was no dog. That was a lion."

"Well, what was it acting like a dog for? I hate it when I don't get a good night's sleep."

The Africans are still telling stories about Ken Kelman.

- How do you think Kelman feels about animals? What is his attitude toward wild animals?
- Do you think Kelman had a good time?
- What would you like to know about Kelman and his friend (the author)? Write down at least five questions that you have about the story.

Appendix E: Home Group Discussion Questions

Directions: Tell your group members about your section of the story. Person 1 goes first. Be sure to ask questions if there is something you do not understand. Take notes below.

When you are finished discuss the questions below.

- What is Kelman's life style like?
- Why did the author take Kelman on a hike along the Appalachian Trail?
- What happened on the hike?
- Why are Africans still telling stories about Kelman?
- What is the tone of this story (e.g., serious, humorous)? What makes you feel this way?
- What kind of person do you think Kelman is? Describe him.
- Do you think people—like Kelman—who never visit nature, would want to go to a place like Africa? Why or why not?
- Why do you think some people—like Kelman—are ignorant about nature?
- Is this a potentially bad thing? Why or why not? Give some examples to support your opinion.
- What are some good ways to get people interested in nature and the environment?

Appendix F: "Schmo of Kilimanjaro" Quiz

Name_____

Answer the following questions true (T) or false (F). Do not look at your papers or discuss the questions with your group members.

1. _____ They went to a game park in Kenya.

2. _____ Kelman loves to take walks outdoors.

3. _____ There are a lot of state parks near New York City.

4. _____ Kelman kept a dog outside his tent.

5. _____ The author is an experienced nature watcher.

6. _____ Kelman makes movies.

7. _____ Kelman saw some cats while hiking.

8. _____ A bear tried to drag Kelman through a fence.

9. _____ Kelman and the author often go hiking together.

10. _____ Kelman chased a lion.

Contributor

Spencer D. Weatherly is an EFL teacher at several universities in Tokyo, Japan. His interests include materials development, cooperative strategies in the EFL classroom, and language testing.

Part III: Maps, Mail, and Other Documents

Editors' Notes

This section is one of our favorites because its authors have gone so far beyond the usual in the selection of their materials. They found them at the Chamber of Commerce (brochures). They found them in the trash (junk mail). They received them in the mail (cards). With great teaching instincts, the authors lead students to read, talk, and write about the issues represented in these documents. We have divided this section into three parts: "Entertainment and Travel," "Consumer Education Through Brochures," and "Communicating With Cards."

◆ Entertainment and Travel
Let's Visit New York Together!

Levels
Intermediate +

Aims
Scan for information
Speak, make
suggestions, and reach
agreement

Class Time
30–45 minutes

Preparation Time
Variable

Resources
Leaflets or brochures
advertising interesting
places in a big city
Maps of the city

Students need to understand the language of publicity materials written for tourists. In addition, planning a trip to an interesting city may stimulate a good conversation.

Procedure

1. Divide the class into groups of four. Distribute the leaflets and maps. Ask students to skim through the leaflets and find the places advertised in them on the map. (See Appendices A and B for samples.)

2. In the meantime, write on the chalkboard examples that illustrate suggesting as well as accepting and rejecting suggestions. Add examples here from your maps and brochures such as *I'd like to go to the Museum of Modern Art, Why don't we go to the Guggenheim? Well, I'd prefer an outdoor location, Well, let's check out Central Park*. If necessary, explain them. Encourage students to use them in the next part of this activity.

3. Ask students to discuss in groups which places they would like to visit. Tell them that they do not have enough time to visit all of them. Each group should agree on only four places and put them in the order in which they want to see them, based on their location on the map.

4. Ask each group to present their choices to the rest of the class. Encourage students to use information from the leaflets to justify their choices.

5. Ask your students to write an account of their imaginary trip to the big city. You may set it as homework.

Appendix A: Sample Map of New York City (Section)

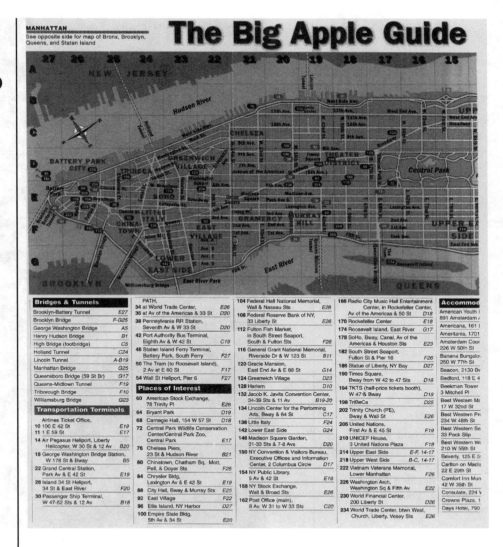

Reprinted with permission.

Appendix B: Sample Advertisement

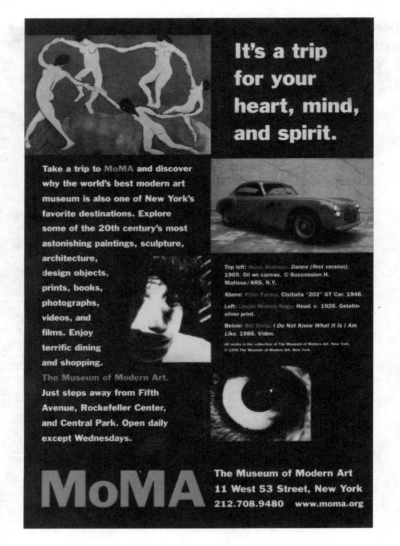

Contributor

Danuta Stanulewicz teaches linguistics at the University of Gdansk, Poland.

A Wild Weekend in New York

Levels
Intermediate +

Aims
Learn how to scan a
text to find information
quickly
Practice cooperative
skills to reach a team
goal

Class Time
1 hour

Preparation Time
30 minutes

Resources
Entertainment section
from a magazine (e.g.,
The New Yorker)
Work sheet

Caveats and Options

Students need to learn to use scanning techniques in their daily lives to find information quickly (e.g., time tables, telephone directories). They also need to develop their social language skills, which include the ability to present their opinions and make suggestions.

Procedure

1. Explain to students that they are going to spend an imaginary wild weekend in New York City.
2. Ask students to scan the entertainment listings in the *New Yorker* (see Appendix A) or other newspaper or magazine to find something that they are personally interested in doing.
3. Have the students form groups with those students who are interested in attending similar events (e.g., sports, music, art, theater, movies).
4. Distribute the work sheet (see Appendix B) and have students complete it as a group.
5. Ask each group to select a representative who will try to persuade the entire class that their group's event is worth attending.
6. The entire class then decides which events they will choose for their weekend in New York.

1. Have the students practice imaginary calls (or real ones if you happen to be in the 212 area code) to some of the events to get more information.
2. Have the students imagine that they have attended the event. Ask them to report on whether or not they enjoyed themselves and to make a few comments about the event itself. They can plan this in their groups or choose a spokesperson.

References and Further Reading

Appendix A: Sample Entertainment Listing

The theater, club, concert, museum, and movie reviews originally appeared in the Goings on About Town section of the July 17, 1995 issue of *The New Yorker*, copyright © 1995. All rights reserved. Reprinted with permission.

Kessler, C. (1992). *Cooperative language learning*. Englewood Cliffs, NJ: Prentice Hall Regents.

THE THEATRE

OPENINGS AND PREVIEWS

(Please call the phone number listed with the theatre for timetables and ticket information.)

LUST—From London, a musical version of William Wycherley's "The Country Wife," with Denis Lawson reprising his role as Horner. Book, music, and lyrics by the Heather brothers—Neil, Lea, John, and Charles. Two previews on July 12. Opens July 13 at 7:15. (John Houseman, 450 W. 42nd St. 239-6200.)

THE NIGHTWATCH—Three Irish performers—Anto Howard, Fionn Davenport, and Helen James—play watchmen at work in Dublin, in an encore production of Mr. Howard's comic play. Opens July 13 at 8. (Camilla's, 44 Walker St. 925-9456.)

TWO MEN POISED—Jay Reiss's comic Western, in which two brothers are about to have a showdown over a woman who would rather be in Paris, runs July 13-15 as the second offering in SoHo Think Tank's Ice Factory Festival. The festival continues through August 5. (Ohio Theatre, 66 Wooster St. 560-7387.)

CLUBS

(A highly arbitrary listing, in which boldface type indicates some of the more notable performers in town. Musicians and night-club proprietors live complicated lives; it is advisable to call ahead to confirm engagements.)

BOTTOM LINE, 15 W. 4th St., at Mercer St. (228-6300)—Decent sight lines, great greasy food, prodigiously talented waitresses, and a consistent roster of high-quality acts. July 18: X, the group once deemed "the most influential band to come out of Los Angeles," is back. The band's terrific new live album, "Unclogged," is an acoustic tour through fifteen years of punkabilly treats, and it captures John Doe and Exene Cervenka's off-kilter harmonies as never before. JILL SOBULE, a particularly gifted singer-songwriter, is the opener.

LUDLOW STREET CAFÉ, 165 Ludlow St. (353-0536)—An unassuming basement restaurant-bar, where you can drink cheap and catch live music nightly. Mondays belong to BEAT RODEO, a straight-shooting bar band that plays a mixture of country, blues, Dylan, Byrds, Velvets, and various pop curiosities.

ROSELAND, 239 W. 52nd St. (247-0200)—Ballroom dancing on Thursdays and Sundays. The rest of the week it's another dark, sweaty rock club, with flannel-clad stage divers and the occasional whirling mosh pit.

CURRENT FILMS

(The signed notes are by Bruce Diones, Sarah Kerr, Anthony Lane, and Terrence Rafferty. If a movie has been reviewed in The Current Cinema, the date of its review is given. Theatre addresses and phone numbers are listed on page 20.)

APOLLO 13—Ron Howard's movie is the true story of the manned lunar mission in which almost everything went wrong—so wrong that there was a real possibility that the spacecraft wouldn't make it back to Earth. The movie, like the 1970 mission itself, gets home safely only by the skin of its teeth. Dean Cundey's cinematography is drab, James Horner's score is unbearable, and Howard retards the momentum with frequent cutaways to the astronauts' families, who are, unsurprisingly, mighty worried. But the acting—especially by Tom Hanks, Kevin Bacon, and Bill Paxton (as the imperilled astronauts), and Ed Harris (as a fiercely determined NASA flight controller in Houston)—is sharp and persuasive, and the screenplay, by William Broyles, Jr., and Al Reinert, makes the scientific details both comprehensible and exciting. The film, despite its raggedness, is stirring. In the end, this failed mission seems like the most impressive achievement of the entire space program: a triumph not of planning but of inspired improvisation. Also with Gary Sinise and Kathleen Quinlan.—T.R. (7/10/95) (34th Street Showplace, First & 62nd Cinemas, Park & 86th Street Cinemas, Waverly, Chelsea Cinemas, Ziegfeld, and Regency.)

BATMAN FOREVER—Is that a threat? In the third installment of the lucrative series, Val Kilmer replaces Michael Keaton as the title superhero, and Joel Schumacher takes over from Tim Burton as the director. Kilmer, in a bulging, rubbery Batsuit, looks and sounds like an action toy. Schumacher's direction is coarse and slovenly: the picture has the self-conscious jokiness of the "Batman" TV series and the smudged, runny imagery of a cheaply printed comic book. Viewers who enjoyed the first two films should follow the example of Keaton and Burton and sit this one out. There's some dignity in surrendering to a bat; there's none in surrendering to a turkey. Also with Jim Carrey (as the Riddler), Tommy Lee Jones (as Two-Face), Chris O'Donnell (as Robin), Nicole Kidman, and Michael Gough.—T.R. (7/10/95) (Village Theatre VII, 19th Street East 6, 34th Street Showplace, Gemini, Orpheum VII, Lincoln Square, Metro Cinema, and Criterion Center.)

NINE MONTHS—Hugh Grant and Julianne Moore are a young couple who discover that they are going to be parents, in a comedy written and directed by Chris Columbus. With Tom Arnold, Joan Cusack, Jeff Goldblum, and Robin Williams. Opening July 12. (Gotham Cinema, Park & 86th Street Cinemas, Waverly, Chelsea Cinemas, 62nd & Broadway, and Criterion Center.)

CONCERTS

NEW YORK PHILHARMONIC—At Avery Fisher Hall, Kurt Masur conducting. July 13-15 at 8: A concert version of the 1885 operetta "Der Zigeunerbaron," by Johann Strauss, Jr., with a cast that includes soprano Julia Migenes and baritone Jan Opalach. Beverly Sills delivers a narration written by Andrew Porter.... ¶ July 18-19 at 8: Mozart's Symphony No. 6 (K. 43) and A-Major Piano Concerto (K. 488, with Helen Huang), as well as Richard Strauss's "An Alpine Symphony." (875-5030.)

MUSIC FOR LUNCH—Free midday concerts. At Stuyvesant Park: The New York Percussion Quartet. (Second Ave. at E. 15th St. July 12 at 12:30.) ... ¶ At Federal Hall: Pianist Yoshie Kubota. (26 Wall St. July 12 at 12:30.) ... ¶ At Bryant Park: On July 12 and July 14, clarinettist Todd Palmer and colleagues play chamber music; on July 17, the New York Percussion Quartet performs. (Sixth Ave. at 42nd St. Afternoons at 12:30.) ... ¶ At Battery Park's Great Lawn: The Abri Trio, playing piano trios by Haydn and Dvořák. (July 13 at 12:30.) ... ¶ At Greeley Square: American Opera Projects presents excerpts from American lyric stage works. (Broadway at 32nd St. July 13 at 12:15 and 1:15.) ... ¶ At Green Auditorium: Pianist Francis Heilbut. (40 W. 68th St. July 13 at 1.)

CATHERINE MACINTOSH AND MAGGIE COLE—The violinist and the harpsichordist offer period-instrument interpretations of works by Bach, Domenico Scarlatti, and others. (Frick Collection, 1 E. 70th St. 288-0700. July 12 at 5:45.)

MUSEUMS AND LIBRARIES

METROPOLITAN MUSEUM, Fifth Ave. at 82nd St.—"Art and Empire: Treasures from Assyria in the British Museum." The highlight of this splendid loan exhibition is a series of superbly rendered low-relief stone carvings that possess Homeric narrative power and irresistible charm. In one, which shows soldiers swimming across the Euphrates to escape Assyrian archers, the trees on the bank are as vivid as Matisse cutouts. A small companion exhibit, "Assyrian Origins," displays early objects from the collection of the Vorderasiatisches Museum, in Berlin. Both shows through Aug. 13.... ¶ "Herter Brothers: Furniture and Interiors for a Gilded Age." Fifty works by the preeminent nineteenth-century cabinetmaking and decorating firm; in conjunction with "Decorating the American Home, 1850-1900," which includes furnishings, pattern books, and catalogues. Both shows through July 30.... ¶ The fifty-three paintings, drawings, and watercolors that make up the Annenberg collection of Impressionist and Post-Impressionist masterworks are on view.... ¶ A display of more than a hundred painted-glass roundels produced in the European Lowlands between 1480 and 1560. Through Aug. 13.... ¶ "The Seven Deadly Sins," a suite of paintings by Paul Cadmus, is at the center of a small show of his works (another of which is "The Eighth Sin : Jealousy"). Through Aug. 13.... ¶ "An Egyptian Bestiary," a large non-petting zoo of falcons, baboons, hippos, and ibis, in stone, ivory, gold, bronze, and wood.... NOTE: The museum's roof garden is open, when weather permits. (Open Tuesdays through Sundays, 9:30 to 5:15, and Friday and Saturday evenings until 8:45.)

MUSEUM OF MODERN ART, 11 W. 53rd St.—The design exhibitions here are always fun, and "Mutant Materials," a handsomely mounted exploration of the way recent technology has transformed industrial design, is one of the best. In what other museum could you find orange fake-fur light-switch covers, Nike sneakers, and a baseball glove on display? It's impossible, though, to imagine some of these things in anybody's house. Particularly loathsome is a "seaweed" chair, formed from shreds of fabric in clashing primary colors stiffened with resin and tossed together like a poisonous pasta salad. Many objects, such as a squishy pen that molds to the shape of the user's fingertips, are displayed on a shelf, where the visitor is invited to palpate them. Through Aug. 27.... ¶ "Artist's Choice: Elizabeth Murray." A large show of paintings, sculptures, drawings, and prints by seventy female artists, including Frida Kahlo, Agnes Martin, Louise Bourgeois, Georgia O'Keeffe, Joan Mitchell, and Eva Hesse. Through Aug. 22.... ¶ "Video Spaces: Eight Installations." Through Sept. 12.... ¶ Ten black-and-white photographs by Gilles Peress document the massacres and the refugee camps in Rwanda and Zaire. Through Aug. 1.... ¶ The latest in the "projects" series is a video work and an installation by the performance artist Paul McCarthy. Through July 18. (Open Saturdays through Tuesdays, 11 to 6; Thursdays and Fridays, noon to 8:30.)

GUGGENHEIM MUSEUM, Fifth Ave. at 89th St.—A large survey of paintings by the German Neo-Expressionist Georg Baselitz. Through Sept. 17.... ¶ "Josef Albers: Glass, Color, and Light," a show of paintings on glass, glass constructions, oil paintings, and rarely exhibited photographs. Through Sept. 17. (Open Sundays through Wednesdays, 10 to 6; Fridays and Saturdays, 10 to 8.)

Appendix B: Sample Work Sheet

1. What kind of entertainment did you choose?
2. For what age group would this entertainment be appropriate?
3. Could EFL learners enjoy the event?
4. Where and when is the event?
   Where:
   When:
5. Why do you consider this event a worthwhile activity for our group?

Contributor

Andrea Maeda is an EFL instructor in the English Department of Ichimura Gakuen Junior College in Inuyama, Japan.

Vacation Decisions

Levels
Intermediate

Aims
Practice speaking skills
by explaining a
brochure to a small
group
Discuss the merits of
activities
Express opinions

Class Time
45 minutes–1 hour

Preparation Time
20 minutes

Resources
Wide variety of vacation
activity brochures

This activity enables students to practice skimming and scanning skills with an authentic text. In general, the use of these skills runs contrary to the careful reading strategies many students are accustomed to employing when they approach a text. The format of a brochure is ideal, with typically short blocks of text as well as enticing pictures that reinforce the text and make it easy for students to understand.

Procedure

1. Collect enough different vacation activity brochures so that each class member can have one. It is better to have more brochures than students so that students have a variety to choose from. The brochures can be found in places such as rental car agencies, hotels near popular tourist destinations, or the local chamber of commerce. Brochures with pictures are preferable. Some brochures describe activities, and others describe places. See sample in Appendix A.
2. Introduce the activity by encouraging students to look over the brochures, which you have placed somewhere in the room to allow easy access. Ask students to choose a brochure that they find interesting or visually appealing.
3. Hand out a copy of the work sheet (see Appendix B) to each student and ask everyone to skim the brochure to get a general idea of the activity or place. It is important to set a time limit (e.g., 2–5 minutes, depending on their level) so that students realize that a careful reading strategy will not be useful in this particular situation. Have students complete the questions in Section A of the work sheet.
4. Next, ask students to scan for important information and complete the questions in Section B. Again, it is important to set a time limit.

5. Students should now form groups of three or four, take turns giving a short explanation of their activity, and answer questions from the group. Model for students how to use the brochure as a visual aid when explaining their activity.
6. When all the group members have finished, the group can discuss which activity seems the most/least interesting and why.
7. Finally, if time permits, you can ask students to give a short presentation to the class about the activity they find most interesting. The class could then vote on which activity to do or place to visit based on the strength or persuasiveness of each group presentation.

Caveats and Options

1. This activity can be adapted to a more cooperative and interactive learning task by forming the groups first and having each group (rather than each individual) choose one brochure from several you give them to look over. This way, students will have to negotiate among themselves to develop a consensus about which brochure to choose, as well as to answer the questions on the activity sheet.

References and Further Reading

Eskey, D., & Grabe, W. (1988). Interactive models for second language reading: Perspectives on instruction. In P. Carrell, J. Devine, J., & D. Eskey (Eds.), *Interactive approaches to second language reading* (pp. 223–238). Cambridge: Cambridge University Press.

Appendix A: Exploratorium Brochure Excerpt

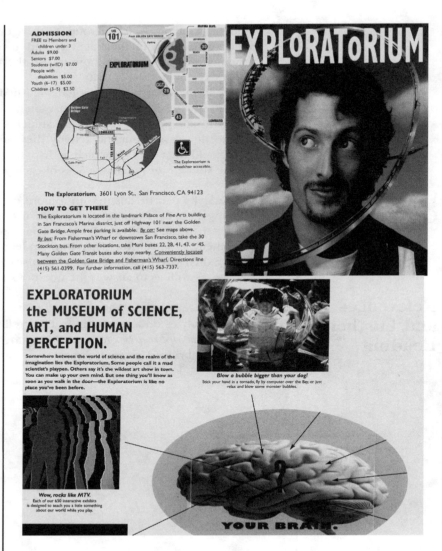

Appendix B: Sample Work Sheet

Vacation Decisions

Directions: You will be given a brochure with information about a popular vacation place or activity. Please read the brochure quickly and answer the questions in Sections A and B below. Next, tell your group about the place or activity in your brochure and answer any questions they might have. Finally, discuss the questions in Section C with your group members.

Section A: Skimming

1. What is the name of the activity or place described in this brochure?
2. Briefly describe the activity or place. What is it like? What can you do there?

Section B: Scanning for important information

1. Where is it?
2. How much does it cost?
3. When can you go there?
4. Any other important information?

Section C: Questions for discussion

1. Which of the places discussed in your group would you most like to go to? Why?
2. Which of the places would you like to go to least? Why?

Contributor

Eric Bray teaches EFL at Kansai University, in Japan.

Discovering National Parks: A Hands-On Approach

Levels
Intermediate +

Aims
Make a phone call and
write a letter
Use encyclopedias, read
travel brochures, and
read a map
Interview a travel agent,
plan an itinerary, and
give a panel
presentation
Write a focused
paragraph to discover
and share a particular
national park

Class Time
2–3 weeks

Preparation Time
1 hour

Resources
Access to a public
library or travel agency
Telephone numbers to
call for information
Encyclopedias, travel
guides, maps

Travel destinations such as Los Angeles, Disneyworld, and Washington, DC, tend to be well known and well visited by international students, but the national parks remain relatively unknown. This project aims to build language through authentic materials while familiarizing students with the U.S. national park system. It requires 6–8 hours of research, collaboration, presentation, and writing.

Procedure

1. Find out what students already know about national parks in their own countries and in the United States. Ask them to name those in the United States that they have heard of and share any information about them. Fill in the gaps in their knowledge by giving some background information about the national parks in the United States, and show a selection of photographs, brochures, and other authentic materials. (See sample in Appendix A.)
2. Give the students information about the project, such as expectations, aims, materials to be used, time frame, guidelines, and grading procedures. (See Appendix B.)
3. Divide the class into groups of five according to your own or your students' criteria. Allow group members time to browse together through the authentic materials you have brought and decide on one national park that they are all interested in exploring. Each group should choose a different park and they should be encouraged to choose a park about which they do not have previous knowledge.
4. Explain that each student in the group must choose to undertake one of the following information-gathering tasks. Allow time for information to be received by mail.

Student 1: Find a travel book in a library or bookstore or borrow one that discusses the national park chosen by the group. Read the relevant section and make a photocopy for each person in the group.

Student 2: Locate an entry in a general encyclopedia (e.g., *World Book, Encyclopedia Americana*) or CD encyclopedia (e.g., *Groliers, Encarta*). Read the entry and make a photocopy for each person in the group.

Student 3: Make a telephone call or write a letter to the chosen national park and request information. When the information arrives, read it, and photocopy appropriate information for all the group members.

Student 4: Visit a travel agent and ask for a map, information about the best ways to reach the national park, and travel expenses. Type the information you find out and photocopy it for each group member.

Student 5: Explore the World Wide Web for information about the national park. Take notes or print out and photocopy any useful information.

5. Ask the students to plan an oral panel presentation lasting about 20 minutes based on the information they have gathered. Explain how to give an oral presentation and how to organize the information clearly. Stress the importance of focus in their presentation. Students need to identify the main points they wish to include in their presentation and provide relevant details to support them. In the panel presentation:
   - one student will introduce the panelists
   - each student will be responsible for giving part of the information
   - all students must be prepared to answer questions
   - all students can choose to present a sample itinerary of a trip to the national park or to describe various aspects of it, and they may include visuals to support their main points
   - all students will have approximately 1 week to prepare for this presentation, either in or out of class time

6. Schedule and perform panel presentations, providing both teacher and peer written feedback. Presentations may also be videotaped for later discussion.

7. Explain the final stage of the project: writing a brochure of the national park. Ask students to extend their presentations into writing a brochure for a target audience (e.g., international students, children, older people). Each group member will be responsible for writing one or more paragraphs or sections relevant to the whole. Ask students to analyze the authentic brochures for items to include (e.g., writing style, layout) , but explain that they must not copy from them. Group members will review each others' writing and ask for teacher input before sharing their brochures with their peers and handing in the final typed project. The group may submit the brochure in newsletter style or as single pages stapled together. These brochures may then be made available to other students and faculty.

Caveats and Options

1. Instead of national parks, choose a different theme for which many authentic and readily accessed materials are available, such as cities, museums, or your own town.
2. To limit the time and scope of the project, concentrate on either the oral presentation or the writing project.
3. To extend the project, have students interview Americans about national parks, invite knowledgeable speakers to share their experiences in national parks, research endangered species, and incorporate videotapes of national parks (available from public libraries) into class work.

Appendix A: Mount Rushmore Official Map and Guide

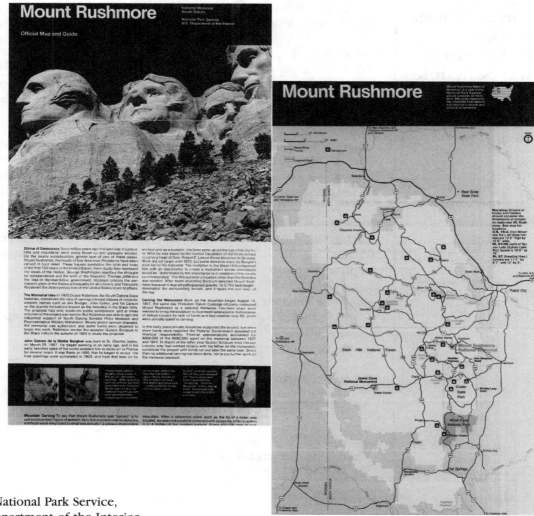

From National Park Service,
U.S. Department of the Interior.

Appendix B: National Parks Project Student Instructions and Schedule

Directions: During the next few weeks of class, you will be working on group projects concerning National Parks in the United States of America. Your group will choose one National Park to research, then you will present your information to the class in a panel presentation and in writing.

Monday, Week 1:

Discuss in groups the information about national parks. Each group will choose one national park to research. Each group member will be responsible for one of the identified tasks. [Teacher: See Step 4, above.]

Monday, Week 2:

Share information gathered with group members. Begin preparing oral presentations. Each presentation should be approximately 20 minutes. Presentations can include a sample itinerary of a trip to the national park and any authentic materials gathered. [Teacher: See Step 5, above.]

Wednesday, Week 2:

Each group will write a brochure of a national park for a target audience. [Teacher: See Step 7, above.] Students should follow these steps to complete the project:

- Decide which group member is responsible for which section of the brochure.
- Analyze the authentic brochures for items to include and layout ideas (no copying, though!).
- Agree on the target audience and write a list of specific items to include.
- Write two focused paragraphs each on specific topics associated with your national park. The two typed paragraphs are due for peer review on Tuesday of Week 3.

Monday, Week 3:

Make group presentations.

Tuesday, Week 3:

Read each group member's paragraphs, checking for appropriate audience and focus. Discuss any possible changes. Rewrite the second draft for Thursday, Week 3. After teacher review, the writings will be compiled into a brochure and distributed to all students.

Contributor

Helen Huntley teaches ESL in the Department of Foreign Languages at West Virginia University, in the United States.

◆ Consumer Education Through Brochures

Save the Environment: Donate $1 Million to Our Organization

Levels
Intermediate +

Aims
Support a cause and argue convincingly for it
Read extended, nonacademic text on a current vital issue
Extract information
Give a persuasive oral presentation

Class Time
1–2 hours

Preparation Time
Several weeks to collect membership letters; 30 minutes to prepare handout

Resources
Work sheet
Membership or fund-raising letters sent by environmental organizations

The importance of using authentic written texts in the classroom is well documented. Nunan (1989) points out that, especially for ESL students, texts such as these provide the kinds of material that surround the student in life outside the classroom. Students are given practice in reading critically for authentic purposes in order to find the real message contained in them. Equally important is the exposure of students to current thinking on and language about potentially controversial issues, such as the need to protect the environment and the role of both government and individuals in accomplishing this goal.

Procedure

1. The key to this activity is setting up the situation clearly. Initiate a discussion on environmental issues. This step may be omitted if the activity is part of an environmental unit.
2. Explain the scenario: An anonymous donor will give $1 million to a single environmental organization. The money cannot be divided up.
3. Tell the students their task: to
   - represent one organization
   - read and extract information on it
   - give a 5-minute presentation on why they deserve the money
4. Form groups of two, three, or four students. Give each member a copy of their organization's letter and a work sheet.

5. Ask students to read the material, taking notes on the work sheet (see Appendices A and B). Group members should work together. Circulate to provide help with vocabulary and other questions.
6. Have one member of each group present. Students may vote for a first and second choice (but not for their own organization).
7. At the end, collect the votes and "award" the money to the winner.

Caveats and Options

1. Continue with a discussion of the function of private organizations in environmental protection, the role of such organizations in the students' countries, and other related issues.
2. Students can be given the texts to take home to prepare the presentation rather than reading them in class.
3. You may want to change the presentation format to a panel discussion where students may challenge their competitors or to a poster format to incorporate writing.
4. You may spend much more time analyzing the language used in the materials. Point out patterns used by all organizations to persuade and to appeal to emotions.
5. The organizations change their letters regularly to reflect current concerns. You will want to keep your supply of letters up to date.

References and Further Reading

Nunan, D. (1989). *Designing tasks for the communicative classroom.* Cambridge: Cambridge University Press.

Appendix A: Sample Materials

Sierra Club Information (excerpt)

OFFICE OF THE EXECUTIVE DIRECTOR

Dear Friend of the Environment,

Let's face it: our environment is now under siege as never before.

Without doubt, the new, incoming Congress -- with virulent anti-environmentalists seizing powerful chairmanships of key committees -- represents <u>the greatest threat to befall America's environment since the dark day James Watt took over the Interior Department back in 1981</u>!

And to make matters worse, the Clinton White House, while somewhat sympathetic to environmental concerns, has not been able to provide the necessary leadership. Therefore, a brutally destructive anti-environment onslaught is quickly gaining momentum and power not only in Washington, but all across our nation!

Often camouflaged under the deceitfully named "Wise Use" movement, these anti-environmentalists are bankrolled by timber, oil, mining and other special interests that profit <u>directly</u> from the exploitation of public lands. And they have launched their massive campaign to keep their blitzkrieg on the environment rolling on. And to keep the profits rolling in!

Their proclaimed agenda is to <u>clear-cut our last ancient forests</u> ... <u>open up the pristine Arctic Wildlife Refuge to oil drilling</u> ... <u>fill in wetlands vital to waterfowl survival</u> ... <u>carve motorcycle trails through wilderness areas</u> ... <u>invite huge construction into our beautiful national parks</u> ... and more!

And the key to their agenda includes dismantling decades of hard-won environmental protection by <u>gutting vital laws</u> like <u>the Endangered Species Act</u>, <u>the Clean Water Act</u>, <u>the Safe Drinking Water Act</u>, <u>the Clean Air Act</u>, and <u>the National Policy Conservation and Management Act</u>. In fact, every one of the landmark environmental laws for which we fought so long and so hard is now in danger.

They must be stopped from perpetrating this catastrophe!

That's why, as Executive Director of the Sierra Club -- America's oldest, largest and most effective grassroots environmental organization -- I am urging you to take two critically important steps <u>today</u> ...

FIRST ... sign the enclosed citizens' petition to President Clinton. It is imperative that you let him know that you -- and hundreds of thousands of other environmentally concerned Americans -- expect him to fight these <u>anti</u>-environmentalists tooth-and-nail when they try to dismantle these crucial, all-important environmental laws and public health programs.

THEN ... when you return your signed petition to me, I urge you to join the Sierra Club by enclosing the most generous contribution you can. Help support the most critical campaign in our 103-year history -- our CAMPAIGN TO SAVE AMERICA'S WILDS.

With your support, our Campaign to Save America's Wilds will ...

1.) <u>Sound the alarm about these "Wise Use" groups</u>, exposing their false scare tactics of "jobs versus the environment," and their outright lies about

Sierra Club
730 Polk Street • San Francisco, CA 94109

♻ RECYCLED PAPER

One Earth, One Chance

National Parks Information

National Parks and Conservation Association

1776 Massachusetts Avenue, N.W. • Washington, D.C. 20036

You may never have another chance like this one.

If you want to see America's National Park System survive, it is *extremely* important you complete and return the enclosed National Survey to the National Parks and Conservation Association *immediately*.

Dear Friend,

If you've visited a National Park recently, you may not be surprised by the severity of my warning!

Our country's National Park System -- the first and finest in the world -- is in real trouble right now.

Yellowstone...Yosemite...Mount Rainier...Denali...the Grand Canyon -- wilderness and wildlife in all these magnificent parks are being destroyed by neighboring mining activities, poaching, overcrowding, forest clear-cutting, oil and gas exploration and other damaging development.

Threats like these -- plus a lack of public knowledge that it must be private citizens like you who must act to save these parks -- can be deadly.

That's why I now ask you to participate in a remarkable new national plan to help save our 80-million acre National Park System. To be a conservator as well as a user of America's most beautiful wild lands and most meaningful historic heritage.

The National Park System touches all parts of our great country -- embracing more than 360 parks, monuments, historic sites and other recreation areas, preserving places and events that reflect the majestic sweep of American land, life and history.

Gettysburg. The Statue of Liberty. Dinosaur National Monument. The striking cliff ruins of Mesa Verde and the beloved grizzlies, moose and Old Faithful of Yellowstone.

Like a living library, the National Park System makes it possible for you to stand on a Civil War battlefield, to walk through a centuries-old forest, to float on a sparkling river that still runs free.

printed on recycled paper

(over, please)

Reprinted with permission.

-2-

Today, the National Parks and Conservation Association (NPCA) is the only private, citizen-funded organization dedicated to protecting, promoting and improving our National Parks,

Over 75 years, NPCA has fought and won battles on behalf of our parks:

- BLOCKING pressure from the National Rifle Association to open parks to hunting and trapping;
- PREVENTING a nuclear waste dump next to Canyonlands National Park;
- WINNING a lawsuit that rid Mammoth Cave National Park of a source of serious pollution;
- PRESERVING the Manassas National Battlefield Park from a plan to build a giant shopping mall on adjacent land;
- PROTECTING the mountain lion in New Mexico and grizzly bear in Wyoming and Montana;

As a result of these and many other efforts, we have won a reputation among government officials, the media and the American public for thoughtful, responsible and effective leadership.

All across our country, NPCA stands at the forefront of national efforts to preserve important wilderness areas, archeological sites, historic buildings, battlefields and monuments -- unique records of America's historic, natural and cultural heritage.

In fact, a group of nearly 70 of the nation's top conservation groups selected an NPCA staff member #1 for his conservation programming efforts, for three years in a row.

But we cannot rest on our laurels now.

Not when aircraft overflight air and noise pollution threaten the peace and solitude of the Grand Canyon and other parks. When Great Smoky Mountains and Shenandoah national parks are being heavily, perhaps irreversibly, damaged by acid rain. When vandals loot archeological sites in America's southwest parks.

And certainly not when development of a proposed gold, silver and copper mines, located only 2.5 miles from the northeast corner of Yellowstone National Park risks degrading water quality, destroying wetland and disturbing wildlife in this remote area.

To combat these and many other threats, NPCA has recently developed a comprehensive National Park System Plan -- a rational, workable program for park protection, administration, conservation and use. A plan I'd like you take part in.

The Plan is the first true long-range agenda ever produced to guide our National Parks into the future...to guarantee our National Parks will be there for the children and grandchildren who will follow us.

(next page, please)

-3-

Our Plan recommends bold ideas like:

1. Establishing the National Park Service as an agency responsible to the President and Congress rather than Interior Department bureaucrats and appointees.
2. Setting more realistic boundaries for nearly 175 of the national park units -- boundaries that will take in all of the resources each park needs (like critical water sources and wildlife habitat).
3. Placing adequately - funded science, historic preservation and conversation programs high among National Park Service priorities.
4. Improving resource management, visitor facilities, education, and interpretive programs.

One of the most far-reaching conservation plans our nation has ever considered, this Plan needs backing from you and many other citizens if it is to succeed.

Right now, NPCA is promoting its Plan to the current Administration... and fighting for a number of conservation bills like the Clean Air Act that will also determine the future of America's vulnerable park lands.

We are lobbying for passage of the Concessions Policy Reform Act to end sweetheart deals and secure higher fees from park concessioners. To save Civil War battlefields. To strengthen and renew the Clean Water Act. For passage of the Old Faithful Protection Act to ban geothermal development near Yellowstone National Park.

As you can tell, our programs are many and varied:

...<u>Budget & Land Acquisition</u>

During the last fiscal year, NPCA worked with Congress to increase the administration's funding request for the National Park Service. In particular, land acquisition and construction at Martin Luther King NHS, and land acquisition at Everglades and Saguaro national parks, and the Greater Yellowstone Area.

...<u>Park Additions and Expansions</u>

We helped lead the fight for boundary expansions to Death Valley and Joshua Tree national parks, establishing a new national preserve in the East Mojave Desert and adding more than 3.5 million acres to our nation's wilderness system.

We fought for and won the fight to expand and upgrade Saguaro National Monument to a national park, gaining it valuable protection from the steadily advancing urban development. And adding 146,000 acres in Big Cypress to preserve the endangered Florida panther and the entire Everglades ecosystem.

Reprinted with
permission.

(over, please)

-4-

... <u>Wildlife Protection</u>

In addition to our efforts to protect the Florida panther, we are helping to save threatened and endangered species such as the red wolf, grizzly bear, bald eagle, mountain lion, and others through habitat protection and expansion, reintroduction, and legislative lobbying and grassroots support. We develop school programs and educate and train park activists, schools, and community leaders to protect critical habitat for endangered species.

... <u>Volunteer Organizing</u>

Through the March for Parks program, the nation's largest annual Earth Day walk event for parks and open spaces, NPCA organizes members and volunteers to raise public awareness of park problems and raise funds for local park projects across the country. One hundred percent of the funds raised by the marchers stays in their own communities for project such as environmental education programs, trail restoration, and historic preservation projects to name a few.

... <u>Grassroots and Regional Advocacy</u>

NPCA gets individual citizens involved through our Park Activist Network by encouraging citizens to write letters to Congress, make phone calls, submit comments, and attend public hearings on park related issues. With eight field offices to address regional and park-specific issues and more than 450,000 members nationwide, NPCA is a strong and effective voice in protecting our parks. Your added voice can make us even more so.

In 1872, Congress created the National Park System for all Americans to enjoy for all time.

Without quick action from us now, you'll be lucky to visit, and recognize, many of them 20 years from now. Please -- join the National Parks and Conservation Association <u>today</u>.

Sincerely,

Paul C. Pritchard
President

P.S.   With your gift of $15 or more you will receive a subscription to our award-winning, full-color <u>National Parks</u> magazine; information on our valuable PARK-PAK with guides, maps, road atlas and travel guide; discount car rentals; plus many other benefits. And -- as a special bonus for joining now -- a sturdy canvas fanny pack to use on your recreational outings. See the enclosed brochure for details.

Reprinted with
permission.

Appendix B: Sample Work Sheet

Save the Environment—Donate $1 million to our organization!

Directions: Read the letter sent by your organization asking for support. Take notes under the following headings. This information will be used in your presentation.

Name of organization:

Area of interest (geographic):

Special focus of work (What do they want to save/protect/stop?):

Past achievements (What successes do they present?):

Plans for the future (How do they intend to achieve their aims?):

Language of persuasion (How do they appeal to you?):

What does the organization want from you?

Contributors

Susan Riley and Salah Troudi have MA degrees in ESP from Aston University, England, and received their doctorates in TESL from Florida State University. They are lecturers in EFL at United Arab Emirates University, in the United Arab Emirates.

Local Brochure Makes Good: Utilizing Pamphlets Creatively

Levels
Intermediate +

Aims
Practice surveying, skimming, scanning, and vocabulary building
Become aware of consumer protection strategies

Class Time
30–60 minutes

Preparation Time
30–60 minutes

Resources
Multiple copies of a brochure
Overhead projector (optional)

Brochures and pamphlets contain compacted information, are available in every community, and are usually written at a high school reading level. They are an excellent, cost-free resource for orienting and empowering international students in their new surroundings. This lesson makes use of brochures and pamphlets as examples of authentic materials which are both readily available and easily obtained. They serve as a rich source for developing a variety of activities that teach language skills.

Procedure

1. This sample reading lesson is based on a brochure entitled *SCAMS* (see Appendix A), which was written to keep innocent people from becoming victimized by scam artists.
2. Inquire about students' personal experiences as victims of theft. Elicit further questions to activate students' background schemata. Suggestions include asking students what methods people use to steal in their home country, or where people keep their money. After this discussion, distribute the brochure.
3. Have students skim the brochure to discover the author and audience. Encourage them to use the picture cues:
   - Who is the man on the brochure and why is he pictured?
   - Why did he write a letter?
   - What are some of the agencies on the back?
   - Why do you think they are listed?
   - What is the purpose of the brochure?
   - Is it to warn or to tell people about something?

   Have students read the front of the brochure and discuss negative words (*don't, con, victim*).

4. Next, have students skim the brochure and determine how the author is trying to capture the reader's attention (format, wording).
5. Survey the rest of the brochure and discuss additional negative words (*lost, jeopardized, ruthless crooks*). Who should answer the bulleted questions?
6. Scan for vocabulary having to do with money (e.g., *financial security, large cash withdrawal, large amounts of money, "good faith" money, cash, cash payment, your account, double in value, financial institutions*).
7. Have students read the brochure. Discuss questions, paying particular attention to the yes answers. Move on to comprehension questions and other types of questions. Where have you seen the name of Attorney General before? What does *in conjunction with* mean? Could another word be substituted for that phrase? What is the swindler's greatest weapon? Why? How can you be safe? What are the warning signs of financial fraud? What is SCAMS?
8. Conclude the activity with follow-up discussion questions. How do swindlers get people's money? What groups of citizens may be victimized most? Why? How can you avoid becoming a victim of a scam?

Caveats and Options

1. Choose pamphlets which are appropriate to the age and level of your students. Pamphlets should be relevant to the local community and culturally sensitive. Be sure that idiomatic language is explained. Watch for length, complexity of sentences and paragraphs, density of vocabulary, pictures, and graphic cues.
2. Vocabulary activities include identifying all negative words in the brochure, or looking for synonyms. For example, students could find synonyms in this context for *professional con artist* such as *ruthless crooks, stranger*, and *swindler*.
3. Consider inviting a guest from a bank to discuss the con artist problem in the local community and to answer students' questions.
4. Students could dramatize several scenarios of possible scams. They could also make presentations to other ESL classrooms alerting them to such problems.

5. To get your students writing, have them (alone or in groups) create a brochure which alerts others to potential dangers from a professional con artist. Have students write and submit essays to the school's publication warning incoming students of the problem.

Appendix A: Sample Brochure

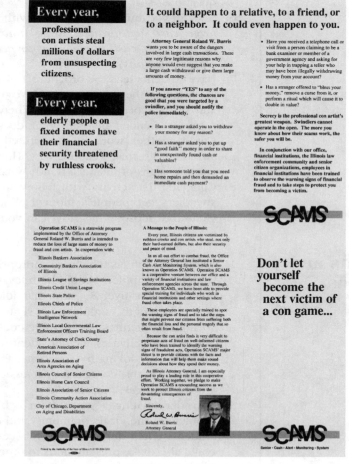

Reprinted with permission.

Contributors

Marilyn Rivers and Catherine Caldwell teach at the Center for English as a Second Language, in Carbondale, Illinois, in the United States.

We Will Declare You Our Grand Prize Winner

Levels
Low intermediate +

Aims
Locate crucial
information quickly
Read and follow
directions
Understand hypothetical
language
Practice task analysis

Class Time
1–2 hours

Preparation Time
30 minutes

Resources
Sweepstakes entry
materials (e.g.,
unopened envelope
with "winners'" names
showing, accompanying
sweepstakes letter on
transparency, official
entry instructions with
each line numbered,
handout)

Sorting through the mail can be a confusing task, and someone unfamiliar with the concept of sweepstakes entries and purchasing incentives may be a particularly vulnerable "customer" due to the difficulty in decoding important details. The activities described below can help students to read and understand authentic materials found regularly in their mailboxes while introducing and practicing "reading to do" skills useful in daily and academic life.

Procedure

1. Ask students to recall if there was ever a time that they won a free prize in a contest. Show a sample (unopened) sweepstakes envelope in which names of winners are listed. How can one tell how many people have already won or how many may win?
2. Using a transparency of the sweepstakes letter, examine the language above the name list for clues. Note the use of the conditional "If you have and return , we will name you as the winner of ." If needed, practice other conditional constructions and note what must be done first, second, and so on to reach the outcome.
3. Provide each student with the official entry instructions, with ordering details (number each line ahead of time) and with a blank index card. Model using the index card to skim the instructions, teaching the students to (a) keep the card moving at a steady pace, (b) focus on the center of each line and "hit" each line twice with their eyes, (c) use a "typewriter return" at the end of the line to "jerk" their eyes to the next line and (d) avoid re-reading.
4. Model by finding the line in which the sweepstakes entry deadline is given. Give students a limited amount of time (5–15 minutes, depending on proficiency) to list line numbers and answers to

important information found in the instructions (see "Finding Crucial Information" handout in the Appendix for sample information).

5. Next, lead students through the steps to take if they plan to order something and if they do not plan to order something. Write the numbered list of steps to take on the chalkboard and encourage them to also write the lists under the entry instructions for a model to use later if needed.

6. Ask students to use sweepstakes entries found in junk mail or provide each with a new sample. Ask students to do Steps 4 and 5 (above) with the new sample (i.e., locate important information and list steps involved if ordering/not ordering).

Caveats and Options

1. You may wish to expand upon Step 1 above by asking students to do a quick write or to explain briefly to a partner the situation in which they won something. Alternatively, you could ask for volunteers to relate their "winning" story, or ask students to read a brief news story about a sweepstakes or lottery winner.

2. With newcomer students needing life skills work, Step 6 could be expanded to teach mail order and postal procedures (e.g., how to fill out an order form; figuring total to be paid; methods of payment; determining approximate delivery date; procedure to follow if dissatisfied with the product; writing a check, address, or telephone number).

3. As an expansion activity to challenge students, you may wish to ask them to decide what they think the crucial information is, to circle it, then prepare a set of questions to guide other students to find the answers. Conversely, for remedial students, prepare a more limited handout than the one given in the Appendix, one that focuses only on dates and numbers, for example, or one that provides line numbers.

Appendix: Finding Crucial Information Handout

Directions: Skim your official entry instructions to find the information needed. Also locate the line number in which the information was found. Work as quickly as you can!

FIND OUT	WHERE?
entry deadline _____	line _____
odds for grand prize _____	line _____
purchase necessary? _____	line _____
second prize _____	line _____
special prize if respond quickly? _____	line _____
shipping cost with $25.00 order _____	line _____
can pay with a check? _____	line _____
how long for delivery? _____	line _____
money back guarantee? _____	line _____

Contributor

Kim Hughes Wilhelm, Intensive English Program curriculum coordinator at Southern Illinois University, Carbondale, has taught ESL and foreign language in the United States and ESL/EFL in Hong Kong and Malaysia.

◆ Communicating With Cards
Be My Valentine

Levels
Beginning +

Aims
Acquire a variety of
vocabulary items and
idioms
Understand the function
of greeting cards in U.S.
society
Identify appropriate
usage of card English,
depending on
relationships and
situations

Class Time
30 minutes

Preparation Time
20 minutes

Resources
Variety of valentine
cards (or greeting
cards), meant for
different people and
written in different
registers

Greeting cards offer students an enjoyable way to look at U.S. culture (often related to holidays), and to understand their customs. Students can experience these cultural events by first studying cards, and then receiving and sending them. In this activity, students familiarize themselves with U.S. culture through greeting cards.

Procedure

1. Put students into groups. Distribute work sheet to students and explain the grid (see Appendix A). Distribute different kinds of valentine cards to each group. Be sure to include a wide variety of cards (e.g., different moods: serious, funny, casual; different recipients: husband, wife, sister, friend, girlfriend, boyfriend). (See Appendix B for samples.)
2. Ask students to look at and read the valentine cards as a group and fill in the grid. Facilitate the activity and help the students if they are having trouble understanding the cards.
3. Ask the students to choose one card that they like and explain it to their classmates.
4. As a class, go over the vocabulary and expressions in the cards. Discuss how the language on a card determines its formality and mood. Also discuss the customs related to Valentine's Day in the United States. Students can compare the customs of Valentine's Day with customs in other countries.
5. Now have the students write their own valentine cards. Some students might need a model in addition to the cards. You may begin the poem for the students (e.g., "Roses are red, Violets are blue . . .") to help them get started. The cards can be written for anyone of their choosing. The students may also write and exchange cards with their classmates.

132

Caveats and Options

1. If you are in an ESL setting, it is a good idea to have the students interview Americans. The questions should be related to how they celebrate Valentine's Day, including to whom they usually send cards. For some students, it is surprising that Americans send cards between friends and families, as well as couples. It is usually very interesting for students to hear the names that people in a relationship call each other (e.g., *honey, sweety, pumpkin*). If time allows, talk about family and partner relationships in U.S. culture. The activity usually increases awareness of U.S. values and lifestyle.
2. You can also use greeting cards for other holidays and customs (e.g., Thanksgiving).

Appendix A: Work Sheet for Valentine Cards

1. In your small group, read the valentine cards you were given.
2. Fill in the grid below.

	Card 1	Card 2	Card 3	Card 4
To whom?				
Formal/Informal				
Mood *				
New Vocabulary				

*serious, funny, dramatic, other

3. Choose your favorite card.
4. Give the reasons you like the card.
5. Discuss with your classmates in a group how you decided the formality and mood of the cards.

Appendix B: Sample Valentine Cards

espresso...the coffee cat...

I can't get through the day without you!
Happy Valentine's Day

Contributor

Mari Toki is an ESL instructor in the Intensive English Program at the Monterey Institute of International Studies, in the United States.

City Tour

Levels
Low intermediate +

Aims
Build vocabulary
Practice speaking by
describing postcards
Practice scanning for
main ideas by guessing
the titles of the
postcards
Become familiar with
the local area by using
postcards

Class Time
20–30 minutes

Preparation Time
15 minutes

Resources
Variety of postcards

An information gap activity is an effective and meaningful way to practice speaking. Since postcards can be easily found in most towns and cities, this activity utilizes postcards as the primary resource. This activity is used as a part of the orientation to familiarize the students with the new area and as a preparation for an excursion. This activity will give students basic information and vocabulary they will need for the excursion. They also learn how to describe what they see at the location.

Procedure

1. Copy descriptions of postcards (usually on the back) onto a piece of paper. Leave the title (e.g., the site or name of the animal) of the postcards blank when copying. Cover the title on the postcards.
2. Put students into pairs or groups depending on the number of students.
3. Distribute several postcards to each pair or group. Different pairs receive different category cards (e.g., animals, nature, scenery, buildings). For example, one pair receives several postcards which are all famous buildings in the area. Another pair receives postcards with wild sea creatures. In this way, matching the cards will be more challenging (see sample in Appendix).
4. Put the description cards on the desk. Instruct students to match postcards and description cards.
5. One student describes postcards by looking at the pictures. The other students choose the correct description card. Students can ask questions to the describer, such as: What is the color of the bridge in the picture? Students underline unfamiliar words on the description cards when choosing. The teacher facilitates and answers questions. Students take turns describing and listening.

6. After matching all postcards and description cards, students consult with one another and write the best title for the cards.
7. Now they can uncover the title and descriptions of the postcards and check whether or not they chose the correct matches.
8. Each pair or group introduces its postcards to the other groups.

Caveats and Options

1. As a follow-up activity, students can make up their own postcards with their own pictures and send postcards to their family and friends.

Appendix: Sample Postcard and Description

Reprinted with permission of Lisa Bryan, The Sketcher Collection.

The Village Corner
MEDITERRANEAN BISTRO

..... has been a Carmel landmark for over 50 years. Dining is relaxed and romantic under the sun or stars in our lush garden patio.

Artist Lisa Bryan - Sketcher® of Carmel 1996© Fax (408) 626-0533

Dolores & Sixth. P.O.Box 2265 Carmel, CA 93921 (408) 624-3588

Reprinted with permission of Lisa Bryan, The Sketcher Collection.

Contributor

Mari Toki is an ESL instructor in the Intensive English Program at the Monterey Institute of International Studies, in the United States.

Postcards From the Edge of Tense, Time, and Aspect

Levels
Intermediate +

Aims
Analyze authentic texts
to raise language
awareness
Practice writing
messages in a specific
genre

Class Time
45–60 minutes

Preparation Time
1 hour

Resources
Collection of postcards
sent from friends or
family

A potential problem for learners is the complex combination of verb forms and time expressions used in native speaker discourse. In natural discourse, learners may not be exposed to a categorically neat usage of tense, time, and aspect. More than likely, learners will have to cope with how native speakers compose meaning according to the context of a situation. This problem-solving exercise is designed to demonstrate the flexibility of language that textbook grammars traditionally steer away from. A postcard was chosen because of the range of verb tenses and time expressions used. Additionally, postcards are an interesting, compact, easy-to-come-by data source that can be used for various activities.

Procedure

1. Gather any postcards you may have saved and check them for grammar points. Look specifically for verb and time expressions, keeping an eye out for how they operate. Photocopy the original postcard and type out the message if necessary so that it can be distributed to the class (see sample in Appendix A).
2. In groups of two to three have students read through the postcard underlining all of the verb forms they are able to find.
3. Next, have students circle any time expressions (e.g., *after, about 4 weeks now, years since*). See sample (Appendix B).
4. Have students place the sender's actions on the space and time line work sheet (see Appendix C) in order to figure out where the sender is, was, and will be; what the sender has been doing and expects to do. Specifically, have students place verb and time expressions on the time line to try and reconstruct the sender's past, present, and future plans.

5. Finally, students should discuss and reflect on the problematic use of tense, time, and aspect by noticing how the sender relays his or her message. Possible issues and questions to discuss might include: Is there an unexpected usage of verb and time expressions? How does the recipient know where the sender is, what he or she has already done, and what he or she plans to do or will do in the future? Is there an overlap in the usage of different tense and time expressions?
6. If time allows, give students the opportunity to investigate more than one postcard from your collection.

Caveats and Options

1. After analyzing and discussing the postcard as a unique genre, students may be encouraged to try writing and sending postcards to friends or prearranged penpals in other ESL classes.
2. Students can bring in favorite postcards they have received from friends and family and share them with classmates in small groups.

References and Further Reading

Bantock, N. (1991). *Griffin and Sabine: An extraordinary correspondence*. New York: Chronicle Books.

van Lier, L. (1996). *Interaction in the language curriculum: Awareness, autonomy, and authenticity*. New York: Longman.

Appendix A: Sample Postcard

Dear Bob, Greetings from Prague, Czech! After finishing up everything in Toulouse, I've begun travels. It's been about 4 weeks now and it's flown by - visited Spain, Greece, Italy, Germany, Austria, & Czech. Prague is amazing - by far the best place I visited - beautiful & very cheap. Believe it or not, I'm now heading for Finland to spend another 2 weeks. I can hardly believe it's been 3 years since I left Helsinki. I'll be there on the longest day of the year and Katja & Minna have made lots of plans. I head back to the states at the beginning of July. Hope your last semester at UCLA went well. graduation, how! Take care and hope to see you this summer! Lots o' love! congratulations on your ciao

TO: Bob Cole
22977 Espada Dr.
Salinas, CA 93908
USA

PAR AVION!

Prazské mosty • Prager Brücken • The bridges of Prague • Ponts de Prague • Il ponti di Praga

Foto Miroslav Krob
GRAFIATISK a. s., Dĕčín

2,90 SUOMI FINLAND

PAR AVION
LENTOPOSTI
FLYGPOST

Appendix B: Sample Transcription

Dear Bob,

Greetings from Prague, Czech! (After) finishing up everything in Toulouse, I 've begun travels. It 's been (about 4 weeks now) and it's flown by — visited Spain, Greece, Italy, Germany, Austria, + Czech. Prague is amazing—by far the best place I visited—beautiful + very cheap. Believe it or not, I'm now heading for Finland to spend another 2 weeks. I can hardly believe it's been years (since) I left Helsinki. I'll be there on the longest day of the year and Katja + Minna have made lots of plans. I head back to the States (at the beginning of July.) Hope your (last semester) at UCLA went well. Congratulations on your graduation, Wow! Take care and hope to see you (this summer!) Lots o' love!

Ciao,

Lee

Appendix C: Sample Time Line

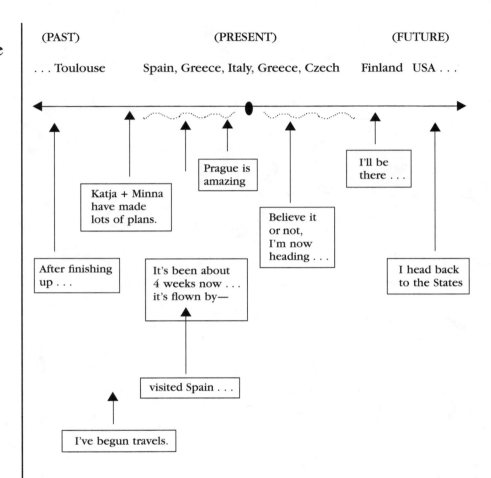

(PAST)

(PRESENT)

(FUTURE)

. . . Toulouse   Spain, Greece, Italy, Greece, Czech   Finland USA . . .

I'll be
there . . .

Katja + Minna
have made
lots of plans.

Prague is
amazing

Believe it
or not,
I'm now
heading . . .

After finishing
up . . .

It's been about
4 weeks now . . .
it's flown by—

I head back
to the States

visited Spain . . .

I've begun travels.

Contributor

Robert Cole is an instructor at the Monterey Institute of International Studies, in the United States.

Part IV: Texts for Academic and Business Settings

Editors' Note

In this section, we pull together a number of activities based on recorded conversations from school and business settings, and several reading activities that might be useful in both domains. The first section focuses specifically on classroom interaction and oral presentations in the classroom, while the second provides an overview of conversational strategies for business (or social) situations. Finally, the charts and graphs section gives students practice with texts that might be useful in either business or academia.

◆ Classroom Talk
Getting Information From Student Questions in Academic Lectures

Levels
Advanced

Aims
Become sensitized to peer questioning in the classroom
Focus on important information in a student-teacher question exchange by assessing peers' questions as to type and by evaluating the content
Compare and contrast questioning in EFL and ESL situations

Class Time
2–3 hours

Preparation Time
1–2 hours

Resources
Transcript work sheets

International students often misunderstand U.S. students' questions and miss information from these exchanges. International students in academic classrooms need to be able to assess student questioning sequences for salient information and ask questions themselves.

Procedure

1. Use the student question types work sheet (see Appendix A) to familiarize students with four different functions of questions. Then, examine how questions are introduced (e.g., What question words are used? Are politeness strategies used?), the important information in the exchanges, and differences between nonnative and native student questions.

2. Divide the class into pairs and have students underline student questions and point out how questions are introduced linguistically, what the important information is, and what the differences are between nonnative speaker questioning methods (indicated by *T:* and *S:*) and native speaker (student and professor indicators *S:* and *P:*) questions.

3. Model the second task using No. 1 from transcribed question-answer sessions (see Appendix B). Identify
   - what type of question it is and why
   - whether it came from classrooms of nonnative speakers (if they can tell)

- how the questions are introduced in each situation (if they can tell)
- what important information there is, if any

4. Students report on their findings or compare their findings with other pairs or groups.

Caveats and Options

1. Discuss where questions are appropriate (e.g., after comprehension checks, during long pauses, when the professor monitors the class).
2. Use an entire lecture transcript to demonstrate the types of questions and frequency of type. This is best done as a follow-up activity.
3. Use authentic videos of academic classrooms to follow these activities for listening for important information from the exchanges, identification of questions, and boundary markers.
4. Another follow-up activity could be writing a short essay comparing and contrasting EFL and U.S. students' questioning sequences for methods of introducing questions, politeness as seen in the two situations, and so on.
5. Transcribing is a time-consuming job, but is well worth it for this and many other authentic model activities.
6. The U.S. students' questions appear more direct and disrespectful than those from international students. This is a cultural issue that must be addressed.
7. What is not in the transcripts is often as important as what is in the transcripts (e.g., visuals used in class and the professor's use of voice cues for indicating importance of information such as duration, stress, and pauses). This can be discussed using a video of the class interaction in place of the transcript.
8. The transcripts have been formatted for this article in ASCII on diskette. Formatting takes time, and if students can be trained to use unformatted ASCII, time is saved.

References and Further Reading

Anderson-Mejias, P. L. (1986). English for academic listening: Teaching the skills associated with listening to extended discourse. *Foreign Language Annals, 19,* 391–398.

Flowerdew, J. L. (1992). Salience in the performance of one speech act: The case of definitions. *Discourse Processes, 15,* 165–181.

Acknowledgments

The system of analysis of student questions is based on Anderson-Mejias (1986). The transcripts are used with permission of the professors at Utah State University, except for those done by Chris Arden-Close and Robert Griffiths, at Sultan Qaboos University, and are archived in CALL Interest Section of TESOL, MS-DOS Users Group of CALL. The transcripts were done by Chris Arden-Close and Robert Griffiths and are archived in CALL Interest Section of TESOL, MS-DOS Users Group of CALL.

Appendix A: Student Work Sheet 1

Transcripts of Student Questions

1. Clarification: The student does not understand and is asking for explanation again.

Nonnative

Excerpt 1

S: What about the insects?
T: The insects come . . . they're animal. They're in the animal kingdom. So the first division is the kingdom (inaudible) put

Excerpt 2

S: Why?
    Why you didn't give the our mountain's name?
T: Give?
S: Our mountain's name?
T: Well well you could do. They could do cert- . . . many many species have a name which is after the country or the area which it lives. It's . . . It's got to have one name; it can either be after the person who collected it or after the area it comes from.

Native

Excerpt 3

P: Okay?
S: Could you go through that again?

Excerpt 4

S: I have one question about the lab quiz, you said there was a disk in there'll be a . . .

P: Yeah. For the lab quiz, if you want to see a sample lab quiz go to the back desk and tell them you want to check out a CS101 sample quiz. It is in the file cabinet in a white envelope. There are about 15 of them in white envelopes, so if the consultant doesn't know what you're talking about tell them to look in the file cabinet, it says CS101.

2. Interpretation Check: This is the rephrasing of information by the student and the teacher either saying yes or no and, if no, reexplaining the information.

Nonnative

Excerpt 5

S: Uh if uh if the orbital uh half uh . . .

T: Half-filled.

S: Yes. So it have the lowest energy or the greatest energy?

T: Lower energy than you might expect.

S: Lower.

T: Uh the energy is slightly lower if it is half-filled.

S: Yes.

T: All right? And if it were higher energy it would not go there.

Excerpt 6

S: Sir uh. The scientist called taxonomist?

T: The scientist is called a taxonomist. Who studies taxonomy.

Native

Excerpt 7

S: This e-cell that you're measuring, that's a value that's higher or lower than what the standard cell is? Like if you could measure a standard cell, what would you give on the . . .

P: Well, the way you would measure a standard cell. A standard cell, standard conditions which means every concentration of electrolytes are one molar. So if I had one molar lead here, then what I would measure here would be my standard.

S: That would be .126 volts. Okay, so then, now you're measuring the e of the cell and it's coming up with a different value than that, right?

P: That's right.

Excerpt 8

S: So the instructions like where the printer operation is in another object code and those are combined . . .

P: Right, and those are combined with this linking operation. Now, in some compilers it's necessary most compilers it's necessary for you to give separate instructions, one instruction to do the translation, a second instruction to do the link.

3. Digression: This is a question that moves the professor off topic.

Nonnative

Excerpt 9

T: Okay. This goat an' a camel can't breed with each other but a goat can breed with a goat an' a camel can breed with another camel and the species is perpetuated from generation to generation because they can breed with each other.

S: Where is the donkey?

T: Well I'll come on to that. If you take a goat from your country and you take a goat from uh . . .

S: England.

T: England or Australia. Then you can still get baby goats from them.

Native

Excerpt 10

S: What was the name of that movie that had a scene like this in it?

4. Correction: This is to correct a professor's mistake.

Nonnative

Excerpt 11

S: Excuse me sir.
T: Yes?
S: So they have higher . . .
T: Melting. Sorry. Beg your pardon I I've used one of my abbreviations.

Native

Excerpt 12

P: And so then we have an equation that we use to determine what
     the resistance of certain piece of wire or material is.
S: Shouldn't that copper wire be .67 to the . . .
P: I probably pulled the wrong one out. Now, it's got to be less than
     Aluminum. What's Aluminum?

Appendix B: Student Work Sheet 2

Task

Transcripts. In the following segments:
- label the type of question asked by the students and be ready to give reasons
- indicate whether it came from native speaker classrooms or nonnative speaker classrooms (if you can tell)
- tell how the student questions are introduced in each situation
- underline the most important information
- circle the introduced word or phrase, if any

One person should be the secretary and should make a table of the information. Your group should be prepared to discuss why you think the information is important.

Be careful! Some numbers have more than one type of student question. This means that you should identify all student questions in the segments.

1. P: Here's my sign convention and I will have, then, the following acting. This is one meter, this is two meters, this is another one meter.

   S: Two meters or four?

   P: What?

   S: Did you say two meters or four?

   P: Oh, it was four. I'm sorry, did I say two? I said two I'm wrong. I've got four there and that's what it is.

2. S: Now, is that 22 on the end? Is that a concentrated force on the end also, or is it . . .

   P: No, it's not on the end. It's located right there and one meter in from the left end. And another concentrated load here of 10 kilonutons at the other end.

3. P: Nitrogen. So if we if we use the dots and crosses method we've already got 6 electrons. 3 each from each nitrogen. So nitrogen normally has 5 electrons and there we are and that's a triple bond triple meaning 3 a triple bond so there were double bond . . .

   S: Excuse me sir. Has the electron 3?

   S: Take out those nitrogens.

   P: Th- this is nitrogen.

   S: Yes.

   P: 3 3 electrons from each . . .

   S: But only uh . . .

   S: This will be 6?

   P: Pardon?

   S: Only . . .

   P: Uh uh each nitrogen has 5 electrons to start with . . .

   S: But that's showing them with 6.

   P: Oh I'm so sorry yes you're quite right I put 3 there didn't I? Thank you. Sorry I put 3 electrons here instead of 2 you're quite right. Ok. Now we don't always want to put all these dots and crosses because it takes so long. So another way of writing this is simply to write it as Cl Cl Cl Cl.

4. S: Excuse me sir.
   P: Yes?
   S: What's the meaning of throughout the crystal? Throughout?
   P: Throughout. Uh Well, it means that if you have a if you have a a crystal the these bonds uh what does it what does it say exactly? Uh wh- extends all it means all the way through you have a single cry-. Imagine we've got a a diamond crystal that big that'd be worth a lot of money. Ha. Ha. But all the bonds go all the way through no matter how big the crystal the bonds go all the way through.

5. S: You don't have to take into account the width, of the. . .
   P: You mean into or out of the board?
   S: The width of the dam?
   P: Well, yeah. That's a pressure, okay? I'm talking in pressure now. If I want to use, if I want to look at a force . . .
   S: Oh, okay.

6. P: I'll give you one example. You take the hydrogen electrode which is a platinum electrode, you pump hydrogen gas in and we have hydrogen ions. . . .
   S: Excuse me, what is the problem about?
   P: Pardon me?
   S: What are we trying to find?
   P: I'm going to find an ion concentration. That's supposed to be my salt bridge.

7. S: Uh what about the fourth electron in the carbon? There are 3 bonds.
   P: That's right. The the i- in a- all the all these 4 electron uh the 4 electrons in the uh here.

8. S: About the one that's down
   P: Here?
   S: Yes.
   P: The the the the uh electron go goes round uh uh the they're each one goes round the each of these rings. They're they're free to move the fourth electron is free to move around the ring.
   S: So that's a conductor?
   P: Yes, it is. That's a g- that's a very good point. It is a conductor but it only conducts along the sheets it can't conduct across the sheets. That's a very good point.

9. P: This one in front of you is a typical figure in Scott's that shows you Horton's law of stream order number, only his looks like, doesn't his look like this?
   S: Yes.
   P: I think his is upside down this may be reversed from that I think his looks like that I think that's right. A stream drainage pattern that looks like this in your textbooks is called Dendritic. In front of you is Figure 16, uh oh, is that a 7? How will you identify it? It's identified by the bifurcation of streams.
   S: What's that?
   P: What's that?
   S: What do you mean by that?
   P: The separation or dividing of streams.
   S: Separation of streams?
   P: That's right.

10. P: So I'll use a full line there. Uh full line there. And if we have another if we have another hydrogen atom here like this those are lone pairs again. These this with a delta plus these are that's a delta minus there. So we get a hydrogen bond between that negative end and this positive hydrogen here. Ok?
    S: Excuse me.
    P: Yes?
    S: What happen to the atom of hydrogen both sides and . . .

P: Yeah. Well the yes the uh that's good th- these these will join up with another another pair here. Ok? Now uh these are fairly these are not very strong bonds. So how do we (inaudible) and in water because water is a liquid at room temperature . . . the . . . you're not because it's a liquid the molecules must be uh free to move over one another. So they are they are always breaking these bonds and reforming them breaking them and reforming them.

Contributor

Jim Bame is a principal lecturer at Utah State University, in the United States. His interests are interactional and transactional conversation analysis, task-based language learning, and discourse analysis.

Getting Information From Teacher Questions in Academic Lectures

Levels
Advanced

Aims
Assess teacher
questioning
Focus on important
information in
questioning sequences

Class Time
45 minutes–1 hour

Preparation Time
1–2 hours

Resources
Work sheets
Overhead projector and
transparencies

Types of questions teachers employ vary in intent and use, such as making students feel comfortable, analyzing data, and clarifying students' thoughts about a topic. Students often misunderstand teachers' questions and subsequently miss important information in these exchanges.

Procedure

1. Distribute transcripts of classroom interaction that are rich with teacher questions (see Appendix A). Make sure the students understand the definitions of the types of questions in Work Sheet 1. Go through the definitions and have the students underline the teacher questions. Discuss their functions.
2. Show a transparency with the types of questions and the short explanations. Divide the students into pairs or small groups, assigning various items from the transcripts in Appendix B to each group. Make sure each item is analyzed by at least two groups. Each group should identify:
   - what type of question is asked and some possible explanations for their choice
   - what important information is being highlighted
   - how they would organize their notes for this class
3. Students can compare their findings with other groups or report on their findings to the large group for discussion.

Caveats and Options

1. Cutting the transcripts into strips containing one number and giving each group only a strip would save paper and could be used successfully in large classes.
2. Using an entire transcript of a lecture can demonstrate the types of questions and frequency of type. This is best done as a follow-up activity.
3. What is not in the transcripts is often as important as what is in the transcripts, for example, visuals used in class and the professor's use of voice cues for indicating importance of information such as duration, stress, and pauses. Thus, use of authentic videos of academic classrooms can follow this for listening to the questions for important information.
4. Another follow-up activity could be writing a page comparing and contrasting the student's home country's teachers' questioning methods with the transcripts.
5. Transcribing is a time-consuming job, but is well worth it for this and other activities.
6. The transcripts used here are from an EFL environment. Transcripts from an ESL classroom environment do not alter the activity types.

Acknowledgments

The system of analysis of student questions is loosely based on Wilen (1994). The transcripts were done by Chris Arden-Close and Robert Griffiths at Sultan Qaboos University and are archived in CALL Interest Section of TESOL, MS-DOS Users Group of CALL.

References and Further Reading

Wilen, W. W. (1994). The theory and reality of instructional conversations for ESL classrooms. *MEXTESOL Journal, 18*(1), pp. 7–20.

Appendix A: Student Work Sheet 1

Transcripts

Here are some examples of actual questions and answers from U.S. classrooms. They are from chemistry lectures. These questions are used to clarify the subject matter. The teacher is indicated by *T:* and the student is indicated by *S:*.

1. Focusing on and beginning the topic: These start a topic.
    T: Now this is the periodic table of what? What are they? What are all these substances?
    S: Elements.
    T: Elements. The elements and there are over 100 elements.

2. Accessing and using the student's content background knowledge: These may start a topic and also are used as a review.
    T: Uh uh. Well it it uh it's a a wide range of melting points and what that means is that some metals have a very low melting point. Anyone tell me uh that what's got the lowest melting point of all metals? You will have seen seen it I expect in the lab. Can anybody think what it is?
    S: Maybe silicon?
    S: I think platinum.
    T: Not platinum.
    S: Silver . . . silver.
    S: Mercury.
    T: Mercury. Mercury. That's right that's right. Hg. Mercury, Hg. That's mercury. Mercury. That's a liquid at room temperature.

3. Explaining the topic: These are used to expand on the topic.
    T: Now if you look at the table carefully and try to pick out which are the metals and which are the non-metals, you'll find that there are very many more metals or many less than non-metals?
    S: Much less much less
    S: Non-metals uh it's larger
    T: Uh uh. Somebody says that there are a very large number of non-metals is that correct?
    S: Yes. Yes.

4. Asking for definitions of particular words: These are used to make sure that a word is understood. When the question is a concept or idea, it may introduce a topic.

   T: What do I mean by empirical?
   S: Like reason.
   T: What?
   S: Existing in reason.
   T: No. No.
   S: Discovered by experiment.
   T: Thank you. That was right. Discovered by experiment.

5. Promoting students' thinking about the topic by involving students in extending the topic or solving a problem. These are used to have the students actively interested in the topic's content.

   T: All right. Let's see if that's correct. Uh now if we look at the periodic table what is there in group 1?
   S: Metals.
   T: This big block here?
   S: Non-metals.
   T: Uh uh . . . they're all metals they're all metals those what about these?
   S: Transition. . .transition
   T: Yeah they're all. . . .
   S: Metals.
   T: Metals. What about those?
   S: Metals.
   T: Metals. What about all these?
   S: Non-metals.
   T: Non-metals. Do which have we got more of . . . metals?
   S: Metals.
   T: Metals. Aren't there? And even in that block if you look at group 3, you'll find that they're all metals except boron, aluminum, gallium, indium, thallium . . . all metals.

6. Promoting students' explaining and defending their statements about a topic: These are used so that the students can verbalize their ideas better and so that the professor can understand their ideas and evaluate their validity and appropriateness.

    T: Sorry?
    S: (inaudible) In water we have a positive charge it it..
    T: Positive charge. What does that mean?
    S: (inaudible) polar (inaudible)
    T: Polar? No. No.
    S: (inaudible) give her (inaudible)
    T: Why has it got a positive charge?
    S: Electrons acceptor.
    T: Yes. But what is the difference between that and that what's the actual real difference? What why is that nitrogen and that carbon?
    S: Because nitrogen acceptor
    T: Sorry?
    S: Acceptor.
    T: No. There's just 1 more proton in the nucleus here. Ok? Carbon has a nuclear charge of s- plus 6 nitrogen has a nuclear charge of plus 7. I think there might be a neutron too, but that's beside the point the difference between these is simply 1 proton in the nucleus and that has no effect whatever on the shape because the shape is determined by the outer shell of electrons and so the ammonium cation is exactly like methane.

7. Students finishing a professor's sentence with information: Students often provide information for the professor as she/he talks. A longer pause in an incomplete sentence usually indicates that it is proper to add the information.

    T: Now there are two types of elements. They are . . .
    S: Non non-metal and metal.
    T: Non-metals. Non-metals and metals.

Appendix B: Student Work Sheet 2

Directions: For the following, identify what type of question is used and why. You should be ready to discuss your findings and reasons for your choices afterwards. Be careful! Some numbers have more than one type of question in them. Analyze all of them. Put the number of the question type from the list below.

    1. Focus/Begin Topic
    2. Use Student Background Knowledge
    3. Explain Topic
    4. Ask for Definition
    5. Promote Student Thinking/Extend the Topic
    6. Ask for Explanation
    7. Fill in the Blank

1. T: But some ions can be predicted reasonably accurately. What do we mean by "reasonably" in this?
   S: By the mind.
   T: Uh not quite. Uh reasonably means . . . uh Well we could say almost here, couldn't we?

2. T: And those electron pairs want to be as far apart as possible. First of all let me ask you why should they want to be as far apart as possible? Why do you think that should be?
   S: Because they repel.
   T: Because they repel each other. That's right. Because electrons are negatively charged and therefore negative charges repel so they will tend to be as far apart as possible.

3. T: I want you to tell me which one is a tetrahedron . . . anybo- How many faces are there?
   S: Four.
   T: Four. Now which one of these?
   S: Blue one . . . The blue one
   T: The somebody's saying the blue one. That's correct. The blue one is that one.

4. T: OK? BeCl2 what's Be?
   S: Beryllium.
   T: Beryllium. Ok. Let's . . . let's start with BeCl2.

5. T: Does anybody know why they are important? What is special about metalloids?
   S: Because make them from the gas.
   T: Uh uh. Well they they are used in electronics. Uh Silicon is a metalloid silicon and you you've heard of silicon chips?
   S: Yes.

6. T: Now we can go on to the sulphur. I hope you can st- I hope you can all see the board all right. Now we can go to sulphur that group 6 valence electrons 6. And we will take sf6 12 electron. That's right.
   S: Six pairs.
   T: Six pairs. So that's a?
   S: Octahedron.
   T: Octahedron. The uh when we say linear linear arrangement, triangular arrangement, tetrahedral arrangement, trigonal, bi-pyramidal arrangement, octahedral arrangement, and the last one is iodine, I. Which is what group's that?
   S: In group 7.
   T: That's group 7.

7. T: Shared between atomic nuclei. If somebody does not know the answer or doesn't understand the question or something, would you please just put up your hand and I'll try and help you. Sharing of 2 electrons gives rise to a . . .
   S: Single.
   T: Single bond.

8. T: Could we have an example?
   S: Cl minus Cl2.
   T: Cl2. Yes. Another one?
   S: HCl.

> T: Eh? HCl
> S: Cl2.
> T: Cl2. We've had . . . there are plenty more . . .
>
> 9. T: Sharing of 4 electrons gives rise to a
> S: Double.
> T: A double bond. Examples of double bonds.
> S: Oxygen. O. Oxygen.
> T: Oxygen is one. Yes.

Contributor

Jim Bame is a principal lecturer at Utah State University, in the United States. His interests are interactional and transactional conversation analysis, task-based language learning, and discourse analysis.

Discovering Nonnative Role Models Through Video

Levels
Any

Aims
Offer powerful role models to students
Provide information about learning strategies

Class Time
5- to 15-minute video segments
5-50 minutes of expansion

Preparation Time
10-15 minutes of interviewing per person
Time to view and select suitable portions for illustrating beliefs and strategies

Resources
Video camera
Video player in the classroom

Students can become frustrated if they are continually striving for an idealistic native speaker model. Therefore, showing interviews of other nonnative English speakers who have successfully become competent users of English (yet still not perfect) provide students with potential role models. As these models are also talking about their beliefs about speaking English and the ways they learned English, this material can be exploited further through discussion and exercises in the classroom.

Procedure

1. Contact advanced nonnative speakers who are willing to be filmed speaking about how they learned English. Let them know your intention of showing the clips to your students and ask them if they would allow you to show it to your classes. Let them know beforehand the questions you will ask. They are usually more willing to be filmed if you tell them that they can see the video after filming and decide not to have it shown.
2. Video only their head and torso. Ask questions that will have them talking for a while (see samples in Appendix A). It's best if they are talking to someone, not the camera. I usually start the camera, and then sit to one side of it and have them direct their comments to me.
3. Show the volunteer the clip afterwards and ask if they agree to your showing it. If yes, ask them to sign a permission for classroom use form. If no, thank them for their time, erase the video, and find other subjects.
4. View the clip yourself and choose appropriate segments that you want to show your class. Decide on the purpose and prepare accordingly (e.g., to discuss beliefs, strategies, or to concentrate on

more language skills, such as note-taking, listening comprehension, idioms).

5. Point out that even when successfully communicating, nonnative speakers authentically make mistakes, just as natives do; they are part of communication and learning. Noticing that the mistakes of these advanced speakers do not keep them from communicating effectively, finding jobs, and getting further education should be the emphasis in such video viewings. The goal is to encourage students to strive for authentically effective communication, rather than inauthentic perfection, and allow them to risk more.

6. Have students complete Part A of the questionnaire (see Appendix B) before viewing the tapes.

7. Distribute and go over questions such as those in Part B.

8. Show video clips as many times as necessary so students can fill in the listening comprehension chart.

9. Do the discussion activity in Part C.

Caveats and Options

1. In class, the video could be used by having a previewing discussion of opinions given in the video or some development of the language that will be used.

2. Also, the class could view the whole segment at once or chunk it into parts. Perhaps, both viewing options could be used in combination.

3. A task involving note-taking could be devised during which students compare notes to collaboratively check understanding.

4. A postviewing discussion about the ideas and opinions could bring out an understanding of various beliefs and strategies for language learning.

5. The instructor could ask the class, "How would you have answered the questions?"

6. This activity could be used to launch an activity involving research on changing beliefs. (See questionnaire following the transcript in Appendix A.)

Appendix A: Sample Video Transcript

Thanks to student interviewer and transcriber Yukari Kushida. She interviewed the four students in this video in the fall of 1995 and then edited the tape so that their answers were grouped around certain questions. All names have been changed to protect the identity of the participants. (* indicates cut to another person on the screen before the next line.)

Students: Hiroko, Takeshi, Chika, Yuko

Interviewer:	I'm sitting with Hiroko [ ].
Hiroko:	I'm a sophomore student at Nanzan Eibei.*
Interviewer:	Hello.
Takeshi:	Hello.
Interviewer:	What's your name?
Takeshi:	My name is Takeshi [ ].*
Chika:	My name is Chika [ ].
Interviewer:	I've got some questions for you.*
Yuko:	My name is Yuko [ ].

Q1:   What do you think is important in learning English (or any language)? Do you think studying hard is very important?

Chika:	No, I don't think so. Umm. First of all, I think, to have interest is more important.
Interviewer:	Right.
Chika:	. . . and enjoy studying,
Interviewer:	studying?
Chika:	It's important to go to another country.*

Interviewer:	What do you think is important in learning English, then?
Takeshi:	Well, yeah, maybe to have destination or to have goal, like, uh . . . , my destination is, no, my purpose is to have fun, to have fun er . . . with people from other country and uh . . . , I wanna have fun. That's it. So, yeah, when I learn something or learn especially language, yeah I try to have fun and have friend from other country or you know, watching *Sesame Street*, or I don't want to study, study language at desk, on desk.*

Interviewer:	. . . in language learning, any language, er . . . what is the most important thing in language learning?
Yuko:	Important thing? First of all, we should imitate. . .
Interviewer:	Imitate . . . foreigners, your teacher, or your friends?
Yuko:	Anybody who can speak that language—native, or teacher, or friends.
Interviewer:	Even Japanese who can't do well?
Yuko:	emmm . . . yes, sometimes . . .
Interviewer:	And have you got some other . . .
Yuko:	Or don't hesitate or afraid of making mistakes, when you use English language or other languages.*

Q2: How do you feel about making mistakes in English? Do you feel embarrassed when you make mistakes in front of native speakers?

Chika:	Front native speakers? In front of native speakers? Now I don't so mind. But when I was in junior high and high school, I was so embarrassed.*
Interviewer:	. . . even in front of native speakers?
Hiroko:	No, because I'm not a native speaker, it's quite natural to make mistakes and uh . . . you mean in my grammar, right?
Interviewer:	Right.
Hiroko:	So I always think contents is the most important thing, so if I make mistakes in my English, it doesn't bother me.
Interviewer:	So if your message is delivered properly, then that'll be fine.*
Yuko:	That's not true if I say "That's no problem", but I don't care too much.*
Takeshi:	It's embarrassing, but uh, I don't care much, because it's not my language, and yeah, I have been studying very long, and . . . , but uh, we can live without English, so you know, I'm not used to using English. So I don't think it's a big deal. I don't care much.*

Q3:   How are you so motivated to study English?

Chika: Because my junior high school teacher was very nice, and I came to learn English. So I wanted to study English.*

Takeshi: He was fun. He was funny. He always brings, . . . he always brought, yeah, brought the guitar to the class. He played the guitar and, at the beginning of the class, every class. At every class, we sang, he made the students sing, the Beatles song and er . . . .

Interviewer: Enjoyed learning English?

Takeshi: Yeah, I think I did, yeah . . . and er . . . 'cos his personality makes me like him . . . You know, I like his class, I like him, I like his class, then I like English. So I study English . . . , and I became good at English, you know, I could get a high score at the test, because I liked English and I studied. Then I studied English much more. It's like a good circle . . . circulation.*

Hiroko: Well, yeah, I think movies really good. When I was a teenager, and er . . . my English was really bad and I really wanted to speak English because I found an Australian friend. I used to go to the movie theatre with a tape recorder.

Interviewer: With a tape recorder

Hiroko: un huh, and I

Interviewer: so that you could record it.

Hiroko: and I used to listen to the tape at home like thousand times.

Interviewer: Over and over again?

Hiroko: Yeah

Interviewer: So, you memorised it?

Hiroko: I could even recite.*

Q4: Do you think going abroad is necessary to be a good speaker of English?

Chika: It's difficult to answer, but it's one way of being a good English speaker.

Interviewer: So, even if you are in Japan, it's possible to study English?

Chika: I think so.

[We stop the tape here]

Appendix B: Sample Questionnaire

Part A (Before using tapes)

1. Making mistakes in English is OK.

    | —————— | —————— | —————— | —————— |
    strongly   disagree   don't know   agree   strongly
    disagree   agree

2. It's good to have goals in learning English.

    | —————— | —————— | —————— | —————— |
    strongly   disagree   don't know   agree   strongly
    disagree   agree

3. Speaking English is fun.

    | —————— | —————— | —————— | —————— |
    strongly   disagree   don't know   agree   strongly
    disagree   agree

4. It's difficult for a Japanese to become a good speaker of English.

    | —————— | —————— | —————— | —————— |
    strongly   disagree   don't know   agree   strongly
    disagree   agree

Part B (After viewing tapes)

Please put a check under the appropriate person's name.

	Hiroko	Takeshi	Chika	Yuko
Who sang Beatles songs in the class?				
Who said imitating others is important?				
Who was motivated to learn English by their teacher?				
Who found an Australian friend?				
Who brought a tape recorder to the movie theatre?				

Part C

Please give short comments to the following questions:

1. What did you think of those people in the video? How much do you agree or disagree with them?
2. Whose opinion was the most impressive to you? Why?

Contributor

Tim Murphey is an instructor and member of the faculty of Foreign Languages at Nanzan University, in Nagoya, Japan.

What Would You Say . . . ?

Levels
Intermediate +

Aims
Collect data via a
student-generated
questionnaire
Analyze and discuss the
data collected

Class Time
Two 50-minute class
periods

Preparation Time
4–5 hours

Resources
Chalkboard, chalk
Questionnaire sheets

Having students collect their own language data can make them more aware of the target language and provide practice in listening, speaking, and writing.

Procedure

Day 1

1. Explain to the students that they are going to create their own questionnaire about U.S. conversation and culture which will be administered to native and nonnative speakers. The contents of the questionnaire will be common conversations and situations. These conversations may take place at school, at work, at home, or on the telephone. Tell the students that the goal for this exercise is to collect and analyze real examples of how people deal with specific speaking situations. Show an example, if possible.

2. Ask the students to think of situations or instances in which they had difficulty in getting their point across, or in which they were not sure how to express themselves; have them also think of example situations which they may not have experienced but which they are interested in learning how to handle verbally. Brainstorm with them for a few minutes, writing their ideas on the chalkboard.

3. Based on the material you have so far, make up an example questionnaire item to show the students what one might look like. For example, if the students say that they are confused about taking a message on the telephone when someone calls them asking for a party who is not at home, you might put the following on the board:

    A: Hello?
    B: Hello, may I speak to John?

A: I'm sorry, but John isn't home.
B: Yes. Please tell him that Tom called.
A: OK, I'll tell him.
B: Thank you. Good-bye.
A: Good-bye.

For homework for this day, have the students continue the brainstorming exercise started in class. Have them each come up with a few example scenarios/situations. Tell them that if they want to, they can also try to make their ideas or problems into conversations, as in Step 3, above.

Day 2

1. Collect the students' situations and ideas.
2. Outside of class, make up the questionnaire, using the students' ideas and example conversations (10–15 items). If the students have the time and access to computers, they could be responsible in teams for putting the questionnaire together and typing it.

Day 3

1. Pass out the questionnaires to the students. Remind them that they are not to complete the questionnaires themselves, but that they will pass them out to native and nonnative speakers on campus, at work, on the street, and elsewhere.
2. Depending on class size, have each student give one to three questionnaires to native speakers, and one to three to nonnative speakers. Tell the students to mark on the top of each questionnaire whether it was given to a native or nonnative speaker. Give them a few days to pass out and collect the questionnaires.

Day 4

1. Collect the questionnaires. Tell the students that you are going to organize the data that they have collected and that you will go over the questionnaire results together.
2. Outside of class, compile the survey responses for each questionnaire item. There are two possible ways of organizing the responses:

a. Under each questionnaire item, make two response lists: one for the native speaker responses, and one for nonnative speaker responses.
b. Under each questionnaire item, list all of the responses together. If done in this style, the students must try to distinguish between native and nonnative responses.

Day 5

1. Go over the questionnaire responses. If the responses are presented as in No. 2a (above), have the students get into pairs and try to determine what about each response makes it nativelike or nonnativelike. Then, discuss their opinions as a class.
2. If the responses are presented as in No. 2b (above), have the students get into pairs and try to determine which responses were made by a native speaker, which were made by a nonnative speaker, and why. Then, discuss their judgments as a class.

Caveats and Options

1. At an intermediate and advanced level, students should begin trying to differentiate nativelike and nonnativelike speech. Students at this level can begin to move from simply getting their point across to asking a question or making a statement that is more appropriate given a specific context. Students develop a questionnaire (see sample in Appendix A) with items that are relevant to their language levels and needs. This is an activity that will take several days to complete and that should be done simultaneously with other activities and exercises.
2. The students could be people who are/will be living in the United States for a period of time. They should be students who will have independent living situations and will be doing their own shopping, telephoning, and other daily tasks. This activity was implemented with Korean business executives living in the United States for a year to study language, but could be adapted to meet the needs and interests of students in most any situation.

Acknowledgments

This activity was adapted from the *Metatalk* curriculum diagnostic test (Firth, Kaplan, & Martin, 1995).

References and Further Reading

Eisenstein, M., & Bodman, J. W. (1986). "I very appreciate": Expressions of gratitude of native and non-native speakers of American English. *Applied Linguistics, 7,* 167–185.

Firth, P., Kaplan, A., & Martin, K. (1995). *Metatalk Diagnostic Test.* Unpublished master's level project in language testing course, Monterey Institute of International Studies, Monterey, CA.

McClure, B. (1995). Teaching socially acceptable responses in small group competition. *TESOL Journal, 5*(1), 42–43.

Appendix A: Sample Questionnaire

1. You need to make a reservation at a hotel in San Francisco for two people next weekend. How would you ask for this on the phone with the desk clerk?
2. There is a fire in your kitchen from cooking on the stove. You need to call 911 to get emergency help. How would you report this emergency to the operator at 911?
3. You are at the Bank of America and you need to deposit your paycheck and then withdraw $50 to spend. How would you make this request to the bank teller?
4. You are writing a letter to your local Congressman Martin Sabo to lobby an opinion you have about the drinking age. How would address the letter and sign off at the end to make the letter appropriate and formal?
5. You are calling a 1-800 (toll free) phone number to *Rolling Stone Magazine* to order a t-shirt that they were advertising. You need to give them information about your shirt size and place the order. What would you say to the operator to complete this transaction?
6. You call your classmate on the phone to ask about the homework assignment and she isn't home. Her answering machine is on and you need to leave a message so that she can call you back. How would you do this?

These questions were generated in class by Korean students in the Intensive Business English Program at the Monterey Institute of International Studies.

Contributors

Jane Mahoney resides in Boston and is director of the Tufts University Summer English Language Programs, in the United States. Anne Rogan resides in Minnesota and teaches ESL to university students.

Welcoming Our Guest Speaker

Levels
Advanced

Aims
Integrate reading/
writing skills with oral/
aural skills
Develop higher level
thinking skills
Explore a variety of
discourse formats at
various levels of
formality

Class Time
2 hours

Preparation Time
30–60 minutes

Resources
"About the Author"
blurbs
Short speech
introducing a lecturer,
from a textbook or
written by the teacher

The manipulation of biographical information, especially in speaking and listening skills classes, is a standard component of language teaching and learning at beginning levels. However, personal information can also be profitably used at higher levels. In this activity, the everyday format of an about-the-author blurb is used to give the students a manageable bite of information about a person which they then exploit by interacting with each other in various ways.

Procedure

1. Ask students to listen to a short speech and identify the context and purpose of the speech (see Appendix A). Read the introductory speech and check comprehension (i.e., whether they understand that the speech will be used to introduce a speaker at a formal gathering, gives relevant information about the speaker, and mentions the topic of the speech that will follow).

2. Divide students into pairs and distribute "About the Author" blurbs, one to each pair (see Appendix B). Have them read the information and ask questions if they wish.

3. Tell the students that they will role-play an interview between the author described, who is going to give a speech, and the person who is going to introduce him. The information given is already known, so they should prepare questions that will yield additional information. Each partner should prepare three questions.

4. Have them perform the role-play twice, switching roles. The answers to the questions will, of necessity, be from their imaginations.

5. Ask them to use the information they have been given, with the information they have generated, to write a speech introducing the author (either individually or still in pairs). Ask them also to think of

a suitable topic for the author to speak on, to be mentioned in the speech.
6. Invite the students one by one to come to the front of the class and give their introduction speech.

Caveats and Options

1. The blurbs need to be of moderate length, short enough so they can be read and understood in about 5 minutes. Besides book jackets, a place to look for them is at the end of articles in magazines such as *TESOL Journal.*
2. This can be integrated into a larger unit of which the "author" will actually give the speech. The partners can work on both speeches together, then one of them can give the introduction and the other the speech.

References and Further Reading

Khema, A. (1993). *Being nobody, going nowhere.* Kandy, Sri Lanka: Buddhist Publication Society.

Appendix A: Sample Introductory Speech

Ladies and gentlemen, I welcome you here today for our lecture on women in Buddhism. We are privileged to have as a guest speaker the Rev. Ayya Khema. As many of you know, Rev. Khema, though born in Germany, now spends much of her time here in Sri Lanka, at Parappuduwa Nuns Island, a center which she established for women wishing to lead a contemplative life. Of course, she also spends a lot of time on the road, teaching, both here and abroad. We feel very fortunate that she has made time to come and speak to us today about this important topic. Without further ado, I introduce to you the Rev. Ayya Khema.

Appendix B: Sample "About the Author" Blurb

Ayya Khema was born in Germany, educated in Scotland and China, and later became a United States citizen. She was ordained as a Buddhist nun in Sri Lanka in 1979, and in 1982 established Parappuduwa Nuns Island in southern Sri Lanka as a training centre for Buddhist nuns and other women of all nationalities wishing to lead a contemplative life. Part of each year she spends travelling and teaching in different parts of the world, and the rest of her time in residence at Nuns Island. She currently resides in Germany.

Used with permission of Theresa McGarry, Peace Corps.

Contributor

Theresa McGarry is a Peace Corps volunteer lecturing at Rahangala Affiliated University College in Boralanda, Sri Lanka.

Practice for Persuasive Presentations

Levels
Intermediate +

Aims
Sensitize students to
some key strategies
used in persuasive
presentations
Increase students'
confidence in giving
oral presentations

Class Time
90 minutes–2 hours

Preparation Time
Minimal

Resources
Selection of humorous
drawings of novel
inventions

Students learn by doing, and this lighthearted activity is intended to be a dry run in preparation for a later persuasive presentation on a different topic.

Procedure

1. Divide class into groups of three to four students.
2. Give each group a different drawing by an illustrator such as Heath Robinson (see Appendix); or, alternatively, give the same drawing to two or three groups.
3. Give each group 15 minutes to prepare an outline for their presentation.
4. Then select one or two groups to do a 6- to 8-minute persuasive sales presentation (each student will only have to speak for a couple of minutes), leaving 1 or 2 minutes for questions. (See Appendix for sample questions.)
5. During the presentation, the audience notes points (both strengths and weaknesses) on the content, organization, and delivery techniques and also comments on how well the presenters captured the audience's attention, maintained their interest, and dealt with questions from the floor. All these points are then discussed immediately afterwards. This feedback can provide useful input for the more formally assessed presentations.

Caveats and Options

1. As a lead-in brainstorming activity, have a brief class discussion on what categories of information would normally be included in a persuasive presentation and how it might differ from an informative one. These points can then form the organizational basis for the presentation.

2. Teachers could also review signposting expressions, such as *Now, I'd like to look at the benefits of ...*, depending on how familiar these are to students.
3. Another option is to videotape the presentations, which can then be played back to accompany the feedback.

References and Further Reading

Ellis, M., & O'Driscoll, N. (1992). *Giving presentations*. London: Longman.

Appendix: Sample Pictures

Used with permission of Gerald Duckworth & Co. Ltd.

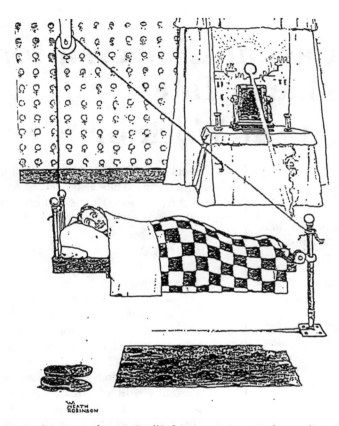

The presentation team has to "sell" this invention to the audience, which will involve conveying the following points:
- the purpose of the machine
- description of the individual components
- how the machine operates
- comparison with other, more conventional means: rejection of alternative methods and benefits/advantages of this machine

Contributor

Lynne Flowerdew is a senior language instructor at the Hong Kong University of Science and Technology, where she coordinates a technical communication skills course.

◆ Casual Conversation and Business Talk

Say It at Work or Say It at Home

Levels
Intermediate +

Aims
Recognize how to close formal and informal telephone conversations

Class Time
30 minutes–2 hours

Preparation Time
2–3 hours if you collect and transcribe own conversations; 30 minutes if you record prepared transcript

Resources
Audiotape recorder
Taped conversation segments
Student work sheet

Caveats and Options

Students need to learn to use promise functions to close conversations on the phone. They also need to recognize native-speaker attempts to close a conversation. They should be able to identify and use formal and informal versions of these closings.

Procedure

1. Ask students to look at pictures (see Appendix A) and guess what the people talking on the phone will say when they want to stop talking.
2. Ask students to listen to taped conversation closings and guess whether the conversation takes place in an office or at home. Play the tape again and have students number the pictures to match the conversations.
3. Now ask them to listen again and write all the sentences that include a promise with *will*. Discuss how the closings often involve a promise to do something or a request that the listener do something.
4. Finally, ask them to write all the forms of good-bye that they hear.
5. Ask pairs to role-play a conversation closing and have the rest of the class guess if they are at home or at work. Depending on class level, you may want to record or discuss how nativelike the students' language choices are (see Appendix B for sample conversations).

1. Do this with other language functions such as greetings, interruptions, or apologies.
2. Have students collect (record) an authentic native or nonnative English speaker conversation and discuss how the functions are realized.

Acknowledgments

The artwork in Appendix A is by Simon Rippingdale, commissioned for this article. Authentic conversations were recorded by the authors and are used with permission of all participants. Names have been changed to protect the identity of participants.

**Appendix A:
Sample
Student Work
Sheet for
Listening to
Real
Conversations**

1. Guess: Who are these people? How will they say good-bye?
2. Now listen to the tape and put numbers under the pictures in the order that you hear them.
3. Write all the sentences you hear that include a promise with *will*.
4. Write all the forms of good-bye that you hear.
5. Role-play a conversation that could take place either at home or in the office.

Appendix B: Sample Transcripts: Closings

(not to be included on student work sheet)

1.	2.
A: I'm going to a staff meeting so could you leave a message up here for me? B: Sure. OK, great, alrighty, bye. A: OK. B: Bye.	J: OK. We will see if it works, and we will try to get this all done the next couple of days. S: Wonderful. J: OK. Nice to meet you. S: Bye bye. Nice to meet you too. J: OK. Bye bye. S: Bye bye.

3.	4.
G: Alrighty, well let me know.	H: I'll let you guys get back to work and I'll see you next week.
K: I will.	F: OK.
G: Say "Hi" to Laverne.	H: Bye bye.
K: And you give a big hug to your husband.	F: Bye.
G: I will.	
K: OK.	
G: I'll talk to you later.	
K: Thanks for calling.	
G: Oh yeah, bye.	
K: Bye.	
5.	6.
K: Right, but what I do is I'll give that to Lisa.	K: OK, and I guess if she needs any additional information, she'll give you a call.
M: OK.	M: Excellent.
K: She'll forward it to Yetta Construction.	K: OK?
M: Great.	M: Very good, Mark.
	K: All right then, Stephen.
	M: Thank you.
	K: You're welcome.
	M: Bye.
	K: Bye now. (simultaneous.)

Contributors

Ruth E. Larimer is dean of language and educational linguistics at the Monterey Institute of International Studies, in the United States. Joyce Kling is a coordinator of the ESL program at The Copenhagen School of Business, in Denmark.

Getting Down To Business

Levels
Intermediate +

Aims
Listen to native speaker
conversations
Create conversations
based on an authentic
model

Class Time
30 minutes–1 hour

Preparation Time
2 hours if you collect
and transcribe your own
authentic conversations;
30 minutes if you record
prepared transcript

Resources
Audiotape recorder,
taped conversation
segments
Student work sheet

Language learners often have difficulty making a smooth transition from opening moves to exchange of greetings to topic introduction or from one topic to another in a conversation. This activity gives learners an opportunity to practice a variety of ways a topic could be introduced.

Procedure

1. Ask students to listen to taped conversations and determine which common features there are in all the conversations (see Appendix A).
2. Ask students to listen to the tape again and determine the topic of the conversation, that is, what one speaker wants to tell the other speaker or what one speaker wants to know from the other speaker.
3. Ask students to listen to the tape for the third time and write down words or phrases used to signal topic introduction.
4. Ask pairs to role-play a conversation in which a topic is introduced, and have the rest of the class listen and write down what topic was introduced and what utterances were used to introduce the topic.

Caveats and Options

1. Depending on the readiness of the students, you may want to discuss formal and informal ways of introducing a topic and how factors such as the relationship of the speakers, the setting of the conversation, and nature of the conversation might influence the way in which a topic is introduced (see Appendix B for sample conversations).
2. This lesson can be followed by topic introduction in a three-way conversation.
3. You may also want the students to bring in their own authentic data for discussion.

Appendix A: Sample Student Work Sheet for Listening to Real Conversations

A. Listen to all the conversations once, and determine with a partner the common features in all the conversations.

B. Listen to each of the conversations and decide with your partner what one speaker wants to tell or ask the other speaker.

Conversation 1: One speaker wants to:

Conversation 2: One speaker wants to:

Conversation 3: One speaker wants to:

Conversation 4: One speaker wants to:

Conversation 5: One speaker wants to:

Conversation 6: One speaker wants to:

C. Listen to the conversations again and, on a separate sheet of paper, write down key words or phrases used to introduce a topic.

D. Role-play a conversation with your partner in which a topic is introduced. Ask your classmates to listen to your conversation and write down what topic was introduced and what key words or phrases were used to introduce the topic.

Appendix B: Sample Transcripts on Topic Introduction

(not to be included in student work sheet)

Conversation 1

A: IEC Mortgage. This is Kent.
B: Kent! This is Richard Andersen.
A: Richard?
B: Yes!
A: Hi, how're you doing?
B: Good, how're you doing.
A: Good.
B: I have two things.
A: Yep!
B: First, Kathryn and I'd like to take the first option that you mentioned in your letter. The eighteen sixteen per month with the rebate.

A: Great.
B: Also, we're ready to lock in the interest rate.
A: Okay.

Conversation 2

A: Hello.
B: Hey!
A: Hi!
B: I wanted to ask you a question.
A: What?
B: Um, I'm gonna go up to Napa next weekend with some friends. And they wanna taste some good Merlot. You have anywhere you can suggest?
A: Uh, only in Napa?
B: Napa or we could go to Sonoma.
A: Okay, uh . . . Ravenswood, uh . . . Franciscan in Napa. Uh, actually their Merlot comes up from Alexander Valley. But Franciscan is right there in Rutherford.

Conversation 3

A: NFSB. What can I do for you?
B: Um, I'd like to find out what sort of services you provide?
A: The NFSB is the premier business lobby for small business. Uh, the service that we provide is testifying on behalf of independent business both at the state and the federal level.
B: Uh hum. Do you have a fee for your service?
A: Uh, we do have a fee. We are a nonprofit organization. So our fee is not set. We leave that up to our members.

Conversation 4

A: Okay, so I'll work on the manuscript this weekend and I should have it ready by Monday.
B: Sounds good. I'll have mine ready by early next week.
A: Good. How many copies do we need?

B: Um, we need four plus one copy for each of us.
A: Fine. I'll have the copies ready.
B: Yeah. Oh, I was going to ask you something.
A: Um hm.
B: John and I often go to Napa, you know, vineyard hopping. I was wondering if you and Jeff would like to join us.
A: Yeah! That sounds like fun. Let's do it.

Conversation 5

A: Denise?
B: Yeah, what's up?
A: Just wanted to let you know, I'm off to a meeting. So if anyone calls, you can let them know I'll be back around three.
B: Okay.
A: Thanks.

Conversation 6

A: Don't forget about the workshop.
B: What workshop?
A: Remember? I mentioned earlier that there's going to be an ACE workshop for women in leadership.
B: Oh yes. I'd love to. Let me know when so I can put it down on my calendar.
A: Okay, I'll e-mail you the info.
B: By the way, when's Pat coming back?
A: Pat? Well, she said she'll be back in the summer.

These authentic conversations were used with written permission of participants.

Contributors

Keiko Tanaka is assistant professor at the California State University, Hayward, in the United States. Michael D'Alessandro works with the Human Resources Strategies Group within Deloitte & Touche, where he assists clients in improving their organizational performance.

Listen and Learn!

Levels
Beginning +

Aims
Listen to how native
speakers use specific
speech acts
Practice those speech
acts

Class Time
50 minutes for each
speech act

Preparation Time
2–3 hours if you collect
and transcribe your own
conversations; 30
minutes if you record
prepared transcript

Resources
Chalkboard, chalk
Audiotape player
Taped conversation
segments
Work sheet with
formal/informal scale
Transcribed
conversations
Role-play cards

Students need to know not only how speech acts such as requests and leave-takings are accomplished, but also the different types or styles of speech acts that are carried out depending upon the setting, situation, and familiarity of speakers.

Procedure

The procedure for one of the above speech acts—requests—is given below.

1. Ask the students to think of how they make and respond to requests in English. As the students call them out, write their ideas on the board.
2. Brainstorm with the students definitions of formality/informality. Included in this segment can be the concepts of directness/ indirectness and cultural differences within these concepts. Identify and demonstrate language depicting formality and informality (e.g., pauses, fillers, modals). Note: For nonnative-English-speaking teachers of English, this part may be more difficult, and could, perhaps, be discussed ahead of time with a native speaker colleague.
3. Design the formal/informal speech continuum with the students.
4. Tell the students that they will listen to three different conversations in which native English speakers are making requests. Inform the students that the conversations vary in degrees of formality. Tell them to listen to each one and determine where the conversation fits on their formal/informal scale.
5. Play the first taped conversation. Wait a moment, and then play it again.

6. Depending on the level of the class and the students, go over the students' reactions to the tape and their assessment of formality after each segment, or after listening to all three segments. Have each student say where they placed the conversation on the scale, and why. Discuss with the students who the speakers may be, what their ages are, what their relationships with each other are, and any other information which may help to determine why they used the particular language in that segment. (You may pass out the transcripts of the conversations either at this step or at the beginning of Step 6. See Appendix A for a sample transcript.)

7. Repeat Steps 5 and 6 for the two remaining conversations.

8. If you have not done so already (at the end of Step 6), pass out the transcripts of the conversations. Go over any unfamiliar vocabulary and answer any questions they may have about the conversations.

9. Tell the students to put away the transcripts. Have them get into pairs while you pass out the role-play cards (see sample card in Appendix B). Have the students act out the role plays while you circulate around the room. When the students have finished one role play, have them pass it to the pair of students next to them. Each pair should get to practice each role play once.

10. If there is time, have each pair choose a role play to act out in front of the class.

Caveats and Options

1. Instead of providing a formal/informal scale, you may provide a direct/indirect scale, or make a scale that combines both of these aspects. Some of the speech samples may demonstrate interesting combinations of formality and directness that may be useful for the class.

Appendix A: Sample Transcription of "Making a Request"

Alice*:	Uhm, I have a favor to ask you, it's kind of, it's kind of awkward for me but uhm . . . I'm moving on Friday and I need to uhmm . . . I don't have a car and I need to borrow someone's car. Wh . . . do you think you would mind if I borrowed your car?
Sandra:	No, that's no problem! When? When do you need it?
Alice:	Friday!
Sandra:	Friday . . . . . . ?????
Alice:	4 o'clock.
Sandra:	4 o'clock? (Yeah) Ok, yeah sure. Well, can you drive stick?
Alice:	Yeah! YEAH!
Sandra:	OK.
Alice:	Thanks, (OK yeah) OK, bye.
Alice:	Hi Mary! How's it going?
Mary:	Pretty good Alice, how are you?
Alice:	I'm good! (heavy sigh) Did you hear about my move? (no, no) Oh, God. I have to move on Friday again!
Mary:	Ohh . . . that's too bad.
Alice:	Yeah, I mean the real bummer is that I don't know how I'm going to do it. Cause I don't have a car, and all my friends with cars are out of town. So I might end up renting a car!!
Mary:	Well listen, don't rent a car! I mean you can borrow mine.
Alice:	Really? (Uhm-hmm) I mean seriously? (sure) Wow (sure) That would be really nice.
Mary:	No problem.
Alice:	That's really nice Mary! (OK) OK, well I'll talk to you later then. (OK, sure) OK bye. (Bye-bye)
Alice:	Hey Nancy, what's up?
Nancy:	Alice, how's it goin'?
Alice:	Oh, you know . . . listen I gotta move on Friday. Would it be a problem to borrow your car?
Nancy:	What? You're moving again?

---

*Names have been changed to protect the identity of the participants.

Alice: I know, I know, I know.
Nancy: Alright, yeah that's no problem, but uhm you'll have to put gas in it.
Alice: Hey, no problem. I'll put gas in it, and let me . . . I'll take you out to pizza too all right?
Nancy: Gas and pizza? (Gas and pizza!) Oh my God you're the greatest!
Alice: I owe you!
Nancy: OK (alright) No prob . . . (thanks) Later!
Alice: Bye!

Appendix B: Formal/ Informal Scale and Role-Play Card

Oral Grammar/Speech Acts
Speech Continuum

Sample Role-Play Card: Making a Request

> You are at school and you have to take a test in 5 minutes. You have forgotten your pencil at home and you need to borrow one from a classmate. You are a new student and you do not know your classmates well. Ask one of your classmates if you can borrow a pencil for the test.

Contributors

Jane Mahoney resides in Boston, in the United States, and is the director of the Tufts University Summer English Language Programs. Anne Rogan resides in Minnesota and teaches ESL to university students.

Real Greetings and Real Responses

Levels
Any

Aims
Become aware of a variety of native-speaker greetings
Practice listening comprehension skills of native-speaker interactions
Get a more realistic idea of how native speakers greet each other
Learn how to respond appropriately to a variety of different greetings

Class Time
1½ hours

Preparation Time
None

Resources
Overhead projector
Two transparencies
Chalkboard and chalk or overhead projector and transparencies
Recorded greetings (optional)

Students have all learned that native speakers greet each other like this: "Hello. How are you?" "I am fine, thank you. And you?" Now it's time for them to go out and find out the harsh reality: that native speakers actually use a variety of greetings. In addition to expanding their repertoire of greetings, students can see firsthand how they are delivered. When students have gathered and shared the different ways to greet people, they may be interested in how to respond if they are greeted in that way.

Procedure

Part 1

1. Define *greeting*.
2. Ask the students to brainstorm different greetings in English (in groups or as a class).
3. Ask the students to brainstorm different greetings in their language (to raise awareness of the varieties).
4. Lecture briefly about the differences between native-speaker/native-speaker interaction and native-speaker/nonnative-speaker interaction, and about native speakers of English and the different greetings they may use.
5. Assign the students to eavesdrop in places where a lot of native speakers come and go (e.g., around campus, student union, dormitories, grocery stores, department stores).
6. Also, ask the students to record or write down five greetings they hear for homework (see Appendix A). Record some greetings to bring in case they forget. When they come back to class with their completed tables, put their data on a transparency on an overhead

projector for everyone to see, leaving room for the responses (see Part 2 of this activity).

7. Analyze the data with the students.

Part 2

1. Pass out copies of the transparency that has all of their greetings on it.
2. Practice the greetings, delivered native-speaker style, with the students.
3. Have the students practice the greetings with each other.
4. Assign the students to try out their new greetings on friends and strangers as appropriate. Have them write down the response. (See Appendix B.)
5. When they come back to class with their completed tables, put their data on a transparency (from greetings activity) on an overhead projector for everyone to see.

Caveats and Options

1. Keep in mind that a greeting, meaning a way to say "Hi!", could include a question like, "How's it goin'?" Explain to students that this question usually functions as a greeting and not as an opening to a serious conversation about their problems.
2. Encourage students to take a tiny piece of paper with them when they do their eavesdropping so they can immediately record what they hear.
3. Encourage students to write things down even if they do not know what they mean.
4. Have the students study and practice which responses are appropriate for which greetings. Then as a kind of pop quiz, call out a greeting (from those collected by the students) and give them an opportunity to give a response without their guide sheets and tables. Other students can help out, comment, or critique.

Appendix A: Sample Greetings Work Sheet

Greetings	Place	Strangers? Friends?	Time of Day

Appendix B: Sample Response Work Sheet

	Greetings	Responses
1.		
2.		
3.		
4.		
5.		

Contributor

Rona Nashiro-Koe teaches ESL at the University of California, Santa Barbara, English Language Program, in the United States.

◆ Graphs and Charts
Comparative Ease With Graphic Information

Levels
Low intermediate–
intermediate

Aims
Develop understanding
of comparatives and
superlatives of
adjectives and adverbs
through visual, statistical
information

Class Time
45 minutes–1 hour

Preparation Time
Minimal

Resources
Statistical information in
the form of charts,
graphs, tables, or other
material that can be
found in newspapers
and periodicals

One of the biggest problems in teaching any grammar item is finding ways of reinforcing the learning through practice. Many practice exercises can be dull and repetitive and appear contrived, and thus fail to stimulate the learners' interest. This can be particularly true in the case of teaching comparatives and superlatives. One way to stimulate interest is to take the focus off the grammar item itself and place it on the content of the task. Authentic nontext materials can be used for this purpose, with learners being directed into using the comparative and superlative forms in order to translate the visual information into verbal form to present to their peers. Especially useful are graphs, charts, or tables that show either synchronic or diachronic comparison of items or trends.

Procedure

1. This lesson assumes prior knowledge of comparatives and superlatives, even if there is a lack of practice in using them. To raise awareness of the lesson's expectations, ask some quick questions about people and items in the classroom. For example, "Who do you think is the tallest person in the room? . . . Will that person stand up? . . . Does anyone else think they are taller than [x]? . . . Let's measure you . . . Stand back-to-back . . . ." Use your imagination to devise questions relevant to your class.

2. Elicit from students two different ways of forming comparatives and superlatives, and what they know about when and how these are used. Illustrate this knowledge, orally or on the board. Be sure to include sentences such as: "There are more [green pens] than [blue pens] on the table." or "More people have brown hair than blond hair."

3. Give students some previously chosen adjectives or adverbs and quickly establish what the comparatives and superlatives are. Some of these might be the ones that you anticipate using in the following activity.

4. As a follow-up to Step 3 and to introduce an element of challenge, put students into pairs and ask one partner to find an original example. The other partner should supply the comparative and superlative. They can take turns trying to score points over each other by finding these examples. Unresolved cases can be referred to the class for arbitration and, if necessary, to the teacher.

5. Put students into pairs or groups and introduce the graphic information on photocopied or handwritten sheets (see Appendix for an example). There should be enough so that different pairs or groups have different topics or different aspects of the same topic. Tell students to read the information and prepare to talk to the class about it. Allow appropriate time for preparation and discussion, then pairs or groups can choose how they will present the information. If the material has been carefully chosen, the presentation will inevitably involve use of comparative and superlative forms; as always, it is important to try to avoid having the activity seem contrived.

Caveats and Options

1. Choosing these authentic texts directly from newspapers and periodicals can be difficult if done just for the sake of this lesson. To make this easier, you can make a point of collecting such information in anticipation of such use. Alternatively, use commercially produced compilations of such information (see References) that, although collected together for teachers' use, still remain authentic. The advantage of this is that often there are several sets of statistics on similar or related topics, so you can plan your lesson to have an overall theme.

2. This use of graphic material could be the basis for a lesson on interpreting nontext material, especially as part of a language-across-the-curriculum policy. It could lead to use of text material for developing critical thinking skills. In such cases, the practice in use of comparatives and superlatives could be worked in as part of the warm-up process, or as a postlearning activity.

References and Further Reading

Department of National Education. (1994). *South Africa's new language policy: The facts.* Pretoria, South Africa: Author.

Foll, D. (1990). *Contrasts: Developing text awareness.* Harlow, England: Longman.

Numrich, C. (1990). *Face the issues: Intermediate listening and critical thinking skills.* Harlow, England: Longman.

Nunan, D. (1989). *Designing tasks for the communicative classroom.* Cambridge: Cambridge University Press.

Appendix: Sample Display of Graphic Information

South Africa's Home Languages

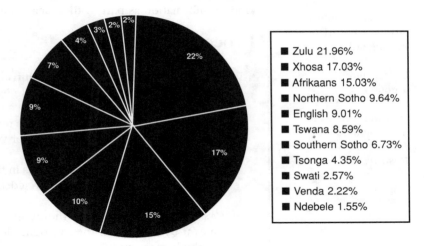

- Zulu 21.96%
- Xhosa 17.03%
- Afrikaans 15.03%
- Northern Sotho 9.64%
- English 9.01%
- Tswana 8.59%
- Southern Sotho 6.73%
- Tsonga 4.35%
- Swati 2.57%
- Venda 2.22%
- Ndebele 1.55%

From statistics given in Department of National Education (1994).

Contributors

Rex Berridge, a teacher educator and formerly an English Language Adviser with the British Council, is now at the English Language Unit, University of Wales, Aberystwyth. Jenny Muzamhindo, a teacher educator and expert in English teaching and the methodology of teaching across the curriculum, is a senior lecturer and head of Communication Skills at Gweru Teachers' College, Zimbabwe.

What Do These Charts and Graphs Tell Us?

Levels
High intermediate +

Aims
Read and interpret
charts and graphs in
academically oriented
reading tasks

Class Time
1 hour +

Preparation Time
30–40 minutes

Resources
Copies of the charts and
graphs

One of the basic academic skills is the ability to read and interpret nonprose information presented in charts and graphs, as they are often used in academic textbooks, journals, newspapers, magazines, and other types of publications. Students need to learn how to read and use this kind of information as part of their academic training.

Procedure

1. Hand out the chart and graph "Blurring the Color Lines of America" (see Appendix A) to students and give them 5–10 minutes to read them.
2. Ask students if they understand the term *interracial marriages* and pick one or two of them (or ask for volunteers) to define it for the class.
3. Ask students to circle the numbers in the chart that do not represent interracial marriages. The uncircled numbers represent interracial marriages.
4. Ask students to interpret the number in each block (e.g., what is meant by 544,000 in the top right block? What is meant by 19,000 in the bottom middle block?).
5. Ask students to look at the graph, and ask them if they can interpret the trends presented in the graph. For example, how does the rate of increase for Asian, Pacific Islander/white marriages compare with that for American Indian/white? Or with black/white?
6. If you prefer, discuss the meaning of the title "Blurring the Color Lines of America," or ask students to give their thoughts on the title.
7. With the above activities completed, now ask students to read the short passage "Tuition Prepayment Plan" and then to look at the

chart Projected Cost & Required Funding For Four Years of College (see Appendix B).

8. Explain the asterisk to students: What are the 7% inflation rate and 6% after-tax rate of return?

9. Ask students about the first two columns of numbers (Child's Current Age and Projected Four-Year College Cost) and see if they can interpret these numbers.

10. Then ask students to look at the last three columns of monetary amounts and interpret what they mean.

11. Lastly, as a topic of general interest, discuss financing a college education in the United States and how it compares with the situation in the students' home countries.

Caveats and Options

1. The central goal of the activities presented herein is to familiarize students with charts and graphs, but the class, depending on size, can be divided into smaller groups where students discuss among themselves what the charts and graphs mean before they present the information to the class as a whole. Other pertinent, similar material can also be used to supplement what is provided here.

Acknowledgment

All sources of information used herein are gratefully acknowledged.

Appendix A: Sample Data 1

Blurring the Color Lines of America*

Interracial marriages have risen dramatically since the 1960s and now comprise more than 2 percent of all marriages.

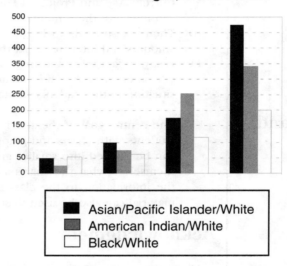

Interracial Marriages, In Thousands

■ Asian/Pacific Islander/White
■ American Indian/White
□ Black/White

Blurring the Color Lines of America*

		Race of Wife		
		White	Black	Asian/other
Race of Husband	White	47,606,000	100,000	544,000
	Black	196,000	3,598,000	59,000
	Asian/other	365,000	19,000	1,764,000

*American Indian includes Eskimo and Aleut for 1980–1992. Race includes Asian, American Indian and Pacific Islanders; Hispanics may be of any race.
Source: U.S. Bureau of the Census (1994).

Appendix B: Sample Data 2

Tuition Prepayment Plans

An alternative to the traditional college savings route is the Tuition Prepayment Plan many state colleges offer. You make a predetermined cash payment—or a series of payments—to the state while your child is young. The state invests that money in a fund where it expects enough interest to accumulate over the years to cover the cost of tuition at a state school once your child is ready. You make the investment today to secure "free" tuition down the road.

Projected Cost & Required Funding For Four Years Of College*

Child's Current Age	Projected 4-year College Cost	Required Funding (Dollars)		
		Single Payment	Annual Payment	Monthly Payment
1	140,250	52,084	4,960	395
2	131,074	51,597	4,817	406
3	122,499	51,115	4,965	419
4	114,485	50,637	5,139	434
5	106,996	50,164	5,346	452
6	99,996	49,695	5,992	473
7	93,454	49,231	5,889	499
8	87,340	48,770	6,251	530
9	81,627	48,315	6,701	569
10	76,286	47,863	7,271	618
11	71,296	47,416	8,013	682
12	66,632	46,973	9,012	767
13	62,272	46,534	10,422	888
14	58,199	46,099	12,551	1,070
15	54,391	45,668	16,118	1,376
16	50,833	45,241	23,279	3,832
17	47,507	44,818	44,818	3,832

*Assuming 7% inflation rate and 6% after-tax rate of return.
Source: Robert J. Garner of Ernst & Young LLP, for *Newsweek,*
April 28, 1997.
Reprinted with permission of Newsweek and Ernst & Young, LLP.

Contributor

Shinian Wu, a specialist in EFL/ESL, trains teachers at Central Michigan University, in the United States.

Reading a University Schedule and Visiting a University Class

Levels
Intermediate +

Aims
Become familiar with a
university class schedule
Arrange a class visit
with a professor
Visit a regular non-ESL
university class
Make cultural
observations of classes

Class Time
2 hours

Preparation Time
2–3 hours

Resources
University schedule of
classes
University telephone
directory
Work sheets
Access to regular
university classes for
observation

Students in English for academic purposes programs need to build skills in using university tools, such as a schedule of classes. Students are additionally interested in observing regular university classes for cultural, linguistic, and academic purposes. This series of activities will introduce students to procedural and cultural aspects of regular university classes.

Procedure

1. Have students fill in the work sheet (see Appendix A) dealing with the university schedule of classes (see Appendices B and C).
2. Debrief areas of the work sheet that may have been problematic for your students, making sure that they understand how to use the schedule of classes.
3. Have students fill in the second work sheet (see Appendix D), indicating two or three classes they would be interested in visiting on a one-time basis.
4. Assist students in locating the professor of their first choice of classes in the university telephone directory. Have students note down the professor's phone and office numbers.
5. Have students role-play a student-professor interaction with a partner in preparation for seeking permission from a professor to visit a class.
6. Ask students to telephone or visit the professor in his office to seek permission to visit the class on a one-time basis. Assist students as necessary in obtaining the professor's permission.
7. Have students observe the regular university class. Have them fill in the observation form (see Appendix E) either during or directly after the class. Allow the students 2–3 weeks to complete the observation.

8. After students have all completed the observation, have them share what they learned from their observation experience with several different partners or in small groups.
9. Debrief as a whole class.

Caveats and Options

1. Some professors may be difficult to contact to arrange an observation. In this case, if the student has several options, he will be able to begin the process of contacting another professor.
2. In many university schedules of classes, "staff" is listed where the professor's name typically goes. In this case, special inquiries with the department in question must be made either by you or by the students.
3. Students may hesitate to visit a professor by themselves. In some circumstances, the students might prefer to do this activity in pairs.
4. Some of my past students have wanted to visit foreign language classes that teach their native tongues. I have found that this does not work well. First, students can be overly critical of the professor, especially if the professor is not a native speaker of the foreign language. Also, because one of the unstated purposes of this lesson is to give students natural exposure to English, visiting a foreign language classroom may defeat this purpose.
5. Writing assignments or log entries are a natural follow-up to this series of activities.

Acknowledgments

I would like to thank Northern Arizona University for allowing me to reproduce two pages of the Summer Session Schedule of Classes, 1995.

Appendix A: Sample Student Work Sheet for University Schedule of Classes

Directions: Using the Summer Sessions Schedule of Classes, answer the following questions:

Table of Contents

1. On what page will you find information about University Services? What services do you predict a university might offer to its students?
2. On what page will you find information on registration procedures?
3. On what page will you find the course listings?

Course Listings

1. What time of day is "Cost Accounting 1" offered? What days of the week does it meet?
2. What is the department, number, and section of the course titled "Humankind Emerging?"
3. Who is the instructor for "Business Comm" (BA 350)?

Appendix B: Sample Summer Schedule Table of Contents

NAU is an Equal Opportunity/Affirmative Action Institution.
UR/G5250

Reprinted with permission from Northern Arizona University.

Appendix C: Sample Summer Session Course Listing

NAU 1995 SUMMER COURSE LISTING
SUMMER SESSION I, June 6 to July 6

SEQNO	DEP/NUM/SEC	CRHR	COURSE TITLE	FEE	TIME	DAY	BLDG/RM	INSTR
ACCOUNTING				**ACC**	(602) 523-5232			
30318	*ACC 255 1	3.0	ACCTG PRIN FINANCIAL		9:00-10:45	DAILY 70	107	BAIN
30321	*ACC 255 2	3.0	ACCTG PRIN FINANCIAL		11:00-12:45	DAILY 70	107	BAIN
30334	ACC 256 1	3.0	ACCTG PRIN MANAGRIAL		11:00-12:45	DAILY 70	203	AMER
30347	ACC 302 1	3.0	COST ACCTG I		9:00-10:45	DAILY 70	203	AMER
ADVERTISING				**ADV**	(602) 523-4612			
37023	ADV 111 1	3.0	INTRO ADVERTISING		9:00-10:45	DAILY 16	TBA	PAVLICH
32411	ADV 310 1	3.0	ADV MEDIA & SELECT		11:00-12:45	DAILY 16	216	LEI
32424	ADV 311 1	3.0	CREATIVE ADV STRAT		9:00-10:45	DAILY 16	216	LEI
ARTS MANAGEMENT				**AM**	(602) 523-4612			
*****	AM 308 1	3.0	ARTS MGMT PRACTICES		TBA	TBA 37	111	YOWELL
ANTHROPOLOGY				**ANT**	(602) 523-3180			
35173	*ANT 101 1	3.0	HUMANKIND EMERGING		9:00-10:45	DAILY 65	317	TAYLOR
36620	*ANT 301 1	3.0	PEOPLES OF THE WORLD		9:00-10:45	DAILY 65	325	RINER
36633	*ANT 301 2	3.0	PEOPLES OF THE WORLD		11:00-12:45	DAILY 65	317	RINER
ART EDUCATION				**ARE**	(602) 523-4612			
32453	ARE 231 1	3.0	ART ELEMENTARY SCH	$10	9:00-10:45	DAILY 37	205	CROSLIN
37007	◆ARE 531 1	3.0	ART MFTHODS/TEACHERS	$10	9:00-11:15	MTWTH 37	215	LAPIERRE
ART HISTORY				**ARH**	(602) 523-4612			
37809	*ARH 141 1	3.0	ART HIST SURVEY I		9:00-10:45	DAILY 37	213	PETERSEN
ART				**ART**	(602) 523-4612			
32495	*ART 100 1	3.0	UNDERSTANDING ART		1:00-2:45	DAILY 37	214	MCLAIN
32510	*ART 161 1	3.0	CERAMICS I	$30	7:00-10:30	DAILY 80	TBA	TIBBETTS
32523	*ART 171 1	3.0	JEWELRY/METALS I	$25	1:00-4:30P	DAILY 37	119	PINKOSKI
32536	ART 261 1	3.0	CERAMICS II	$30	11:00-2:30P	DAILY 80	TBA	TIBBETTS
37010	ART 361 1	3.0	CERAMICS III	$30	11:00-2:30P	DAILY 80	TBA	TIBBETTS
37812	◆ART 593 2	3.0	COMPTR GRAPHICS IN ED	$20	7:00-8:45	DAILY 37	213	CALDWELL
ASTRONOMY				**AST**	(602) 523-2661			
30631	*AST 180 1	3.0	INTRO TO ASTRONOMY	$10	1:00-2:45	DAILY 19	233	MASSEY
BUSINESS ADMINISTRATION				**BA**	(602) 523-5232			
30363	*BA 201 1	3.0	QUANT METHODS		9:00-10:45	DAILY 70	102	COHEN
30376	*BA 201 2	3.0	QUANT METHODS		11:00-12:45	DAILY 70	102	COHEN
30389	BA 205 1	3.0	BUSINESS LAW I		7:00-8:45	DAILY 70	205	PALMER
30392	BA 301 1	3.0	PROD AND OPS MGT		9:00-10:45	DAILY 70	106	OZMUN
30404	BA 305 1	3.0	BUSINESS LAW II		9:00-10:45	DAILY 70	205	PALMER
30417	BA 350 1	3.0	BUSINESS COMM		11:00-12:45	DAILY 70	101	WUNSCH
30459	BA 490 1	3.0	BUSINESS POLICIES		11:00-12:45	DAILY 70	106	OZMUN
BROADCASTING				**BEM**	(602) 523-1837			
32581	BEM 321 1	3.0	AUDIO PRODUCTION	$10	11:00-12:45	DAILY 16	309	MAJORS
BIOLOGY				**BIO**	(602) 523-2381			
30686	*BIO 100 1	3.0	PRINCIPLES/BIOLOGY		7:00-8:45	DAILY 21	265	ALLRED
30699	+BIO 100L A	1.0	PRINCIPLES/BIO LAB	$25	1:00-3:30P	MTW 21	145	GUZMAN
30701	+BIO 100L B	1.0	PRINCIPLES/BIO LAB	$25	3:45-6:15P	MTW 21	145	GUZMAN
30730	BIO 184 1	4.0	PLANT BIOLOGY		7:00-8:45	DAILY 21	256	LIPKE
30714	+BIO 184L A	0.0	PLANT BIOLOGY LAB	$25	1:00-3:30P	MTW 21	129	STAFF
30727	+BIO 184L B	0.0	PLANT BIOLOGY LAB	$25	3:45-6:15P	MTW 21	129	STAFF
30769	BIO 190 1	4.0	ANIMAL BIOLOGY		9:00-10:45	DAILY 21	265	GOODMAN
30743	+BIO 190L A	0.0	ANIMAL BIOLOGY LAB	$25	1:00-3:30P	MTW 21	128	GOODMAN
30756	+BIO 190L B	0.0	ANIMAL BIOLOGY LAB	$25	3:45-6:15P	MTW 21	128	GOODMAN

***** SEQNO number, contact department; ◆teachers' consideration; *liberal study class;
+lab science liberal study class. Independent study, field work experience, thesis
research, and dissertation courses are available by contacting the academic department.

Appendix D: Choosing a Class and Obtaining Permission to Visit the Class

Directions: As part of this assignment, you must arrange to visit a regular university class. First you must choose a class to visit from the schedule of classes. Choose a class that interests you and that will fit into your current schedule. You may *not* miss one of your ESL classes to attend the regular class.

List here three classes that would interest you and that fit into your schedule. Include the title of the class, the name of the department that offers the class, the time and days it is offered, and the professor's name.

1._____

2._____

3._____

You must now ask the professor's permission to visit his/her class once. Follow these steps:

1. Find the professor's phone number and office number in the university telephone directory.
2. Call the professor or visit him/her in his/her office.
3. Identify yourself to the professor and ask permission to visit his/her class on a particular day. Explain to the professor that you wish to observe the class to make some cultural observations as part of your ESL class assignment.
4. If the professor says yes, then you are all set to visit the class on the agreed upon day and time. If the professor says no, locate the professor for your second choice class and go through these steps again.

Practice:

Role-play with a partner to practice seeking permission to visit a class. One person plays the role of the student and one person plays the role of the professor. If you are the student, make sure to identify yourself and state your purpose. If you are the professor, ask the student some questions to determine the student's purpose in visiting your class, how often the student will visit your class, what the student will do there, and other useful questions.

Appendix E: Cultural Observation of a Regular University Class

Directions: Arrive for your class observation 5 minutes before the class is scheduled to begin. As you are observing the class or immediately afterwards, write answers to the following questions:

1. How many students are present in the classroom 5 minutes before the beginning of the class period? What are they doing?
2. When do most students arrive for the class? What do they do? What time does the professor arrive? What does he/she do?
3. What time is the class scheduled to begin? What time does it begin?
4. Do any students arrive after the beginning of the class? How do they behave?
5. How many male students are present for the class? How many female students are present?
6. What does the professor do during the class? Is the class mostly lecture, discussion, or a combination?
7. What do the students do during the class?
8. What happens at the end of the class?
9. How does this class differ from university classes in your country? If there are differences, why do you think this is so?

At the end of the class, try to make an effort to thank the professor. If you do not have a chance to talk to the professor, it might be nice to write him/her a thank-you note.

Contributor

Sarah Rilling is a doctoral student in the applied linguistics program at Northern Arizona University, in the United States. She has taught ESL in the United States and Japan.

Part V: Food

Editors' Note

Most language teachers and learners enjoy including food in the curriculum, whether it is through sharing meals or doing the preparation together. The three contributions in this section, "Who Said Americans Only Eat Hamburgers?," "Counting in the Cupboards," and "Tomatoes, Etc.," cover areas such as food and geography, describing a recipe, cooking, a grammar focus relating menus to recipes, and understanding ingredients in packaged foods.

◆ Recipes, Menus, and Labels
Who Said Americans Only Eat Hamburgers?

Levels
Intermediate

Aims
Talk about likes and dislikes
Become exposed to different
cultural groups that live in
the United States
Offer students an authentic
situation where they can
practice vocabulary related
to food
Recognize order and
sequence in discourse
Practice the imperative form
of the verb

Class Time
50 minutes–2 hours

Preparation Time
1–2 hours

Resources
U.S. cookbooks
Additional cooking recipes
from different regions
Map of the United States
Map of the United States
with food pictures on it
Menus from different
restaurants
Overhead projector and
transparency of your
favorite recipe

The United States is often called a *melting pot* or *mixed salad* because it is a country inhabited by people from many different ethnic groups. This belief provides the context for this activity, which asks students to reflect on sociocultural differences shown by different types of food (Kaplan, 1966). The fact that students talk about favorite types of foods and may decide to present their favorite recipe (cf. Nunan, 1990) and share a sample with the class will contribute to a friendly atmosphere that will result in an ideal learning environment (cf. Krashen, 1981). The learning of discourse structure and grammatical topics (e.g., sequence and order, food vocabulary, or the use of the imperative form of the verb) will take place within the framework of authentic discourse that occurs between native speakers (Cathcart, 1989).

Procedure

1. Ask the students to
   ● arrange their chairs in a circle, and start thinking about their favorite food and favorite recipe
   ● think about the different ethnic groups that live in the United States (in pairs, with neighbor to the right)
   ● form pairs (with neighbor to the left) and ask each other about their favorite food and favorite recipe
   ● (individually) write a list of the different types of food—and the areas where they have noticed them—in the United States
2. Give each student a map of the United States.

3. Ask students to pair with their neighbor (this time the one to the right) and dictate her list to the neighbor who will transfer it to the map.
4. Ask students to form groups of four and try to come up with a more complete map sharing the information that each of them has.
5. Ask them to show the area they come from on the U.S. map and explain the type of food that can be found there (e.g., Monterey, California; old fishing area; seafood and Italian food).
6. Model a favorite recipe on the overhead projector (see Appendix A). Go through the order and sequence.
7. Ask students if they have any questions. Clarify vocabulary, measurements, order and sequence, and imperative forms of the verbs.
8. Set a follow-up activity (e.g., for homework or writing class):
   - Write a list of possible substitutes to this recipe.
   - Write your favorite recipe.
   - Copy the recipe onto a transparency for a lesson the following day:
     ○ Ask students to put up the transparency of their favorite recipe and go over it with the class.
     ○ Explain the ingredients and the measurements. Explain what might happen if you do one thing before the other and vice versa, or if you alter times or measurements.
     ○ Make sure the students are following the instructions and explanations.
     ○ Repeat Step 7 from the previous day.

Caveats and Options

1. This activity could be used either with beginning or advanced students.
2. This activity may vary in time and shape according to what you would like to emphasize. For example, if you have two periods in a row, you could do a "show and tell" with students from one class sharing their favorite recipes with the other class. If you want to emphasize vocabulary, you could use word group activities for ingredients, measurements, commands.
3. If you want to emphasize order and sequence, you might cut sentences and mix them up asking students to order them. Or you

might cut out words and ask students to group them into families of words.

4. If you want to emphasize more listening comprehension and geography content, you might do a listening comprehension exercise on a map of the United States. You may read a piece of authentic discourse related to food in the United States, such as an article in a womens' magazine or gourmet magazine and have students locate the areas mentioned on the map. You might also do a listening comprehension activity with pictures of dishes that beginners might circle as they listen to the piece of discourse.

5. You might use this for a grammar lesson on comparisons if you start asking questions such as: Which recipe is more complicated, the cioppino or the banana bread? Which recipe has more ingredients?

References and Further Reading

Cathcart, R. (1989). Authentic discourse and the survival English curriculum. *TESOL Quarterly, 23,* 105–126.

Kaplan, R. (1966). Cultural thought patterns in inter-cultural education. *Language Learning, 16,* 1–20.

Krashen, S. D. (1981). *Second language acquisition and second language learning.* Oxford: Pergamon.

Nunan, D. (1990). Using learner data in curriculum development. *English for Specific Purposes, 9,* 17–32.

Acknowledgment

Special thanks to my grandmother Elda for being herself and for the love she gave, even through her cooking.

Appendix A: Sample Recipe

 # Cioppino

Ingredients *(6 servings)*
- 1 bottle of cioppino sauce
- 12 mussels
- 12 clams
- ½ pound shrimp
- 4 fresh fish fillets (red snapper or cod fish)
- 1 can of crab meat

Heat the cioppino sauce in a deep pot over moderate to low heat. 30 minutes before dinner time, add the fish fillets. 15 minutes before, add the crab meat and the shrimp. 10 minutes before add the mussels and the clams. Serve it in bowls. Delicious with garlic bread!

NB: If you love preparing recipes from scratch, substitute the following home made sauce for the cioppino:
- 1 pound tomatoes
- 2 big white onions
- 2 green onions
- ½ cup of fresh parsley
- ½ cup of fresh cilantro
- ½ cup of celery
- 5 garlic cloves
- salt, pepper

Puree the tomatoes. Peel the onions and chop them with the parsley, the cilantro, the celery, and the garlic. Add salt and pepper.

Contributor

Claudia Angelelli is an instructor in the Spanish Department and the School of Law at Stanford University, in the United States.

Counting in the Cupboards

Levels
Intermediate +

Aims
Learn and use some
English food vocabulary
Discover a system for
how articles are used
with mass/count food
nouns

Class Time
Three 45-minute
sessions

Preparation Time
1–2 hours

Resources
Magazines, blank paper,
scissors, glue sticks,
menus from restaurants,
recipes
Cameras and film
Computer (optional)

This collection of hands-on activities provides a model for interesting, relevant, and meaningful ways of raising students' awareness of how the U.S. English article system functions in relation to food.

Procedure

Part 1

1. Provide students with a pile of magazines with pictures of food: single items and ethnic dishes.
2. Discuss how articles are used with the food items. Have students try to discover a pattern.
3. Ask students if we can count the food items. If they are mass nouns, are they unit/serving or kind/type?
4. Have groups of students make a chart and place food item pictures under count or noncount (mass) categories.

Part 2

5. Collect sample menus from local ethnic restaurants.
6. Distribute the menus to groups of students (see sample in Appendix A).
7. Direct the students to underline the food words and note the articles used. Ask the students to note any differences that may occur in article usage with food items on the menu as compared with the chart made earlier.
8. Discuss with the students possible reasons for any observed differences in article usage between the words on the food chart and in the menu.

9. Have the students, in pairs or small groups, make a short, menu including photographs, drawings, or magazine pictures of their favorite foods. Share or display the menus.

Part 3

10. Select a recipe from the newspaper, a cookbook, or someone's recipe file (see Appendix B).
11. Highlight where the articles are missing (0 article use).
12. Make copies of the recipe and distribute to the students.
13. Instruct them to work with a partner to discover where articles are missing.
14. Next have them write the recipe out in story form and answer why they think they left the article out.

Part 4

15. Have the students bring in a recipe of their favorite food from their home country.
16. Have them write up the recipe in English, emulating the cookbook model.
17. Assemble a cookbook for each member of the class with their menus and sample recipes.

Caveats and Options

1. This collection of exercises could be expanded to include language awareness activities exploring the kinds of mass/count food words that exist in the students' first languages. A comparison could be done between the various languages and what food words are considered count/mass. Students could be encouraged to postulate why any observed differences between languages exist.

References and Further Reading

Celce-Murcia, M., Larsen-Freeman, D. (1983). *The grammar book: An ESL/EFL teacher's course.* Boston: Heinle & Heinle.

Celce-Murcia, M. (1991). Grammar pedagogy in second and foreign language instruction. *TESOL Quarterly, 25*, 459–480.

Appendix A: Sample Menu Activity

1. Underline the food words in the following menu.
2. Look at the articles used with the food items on the menu. Remember the chart we made about noncount and count food items? Look at the chart and compare. Are there any food items in both places? Are the articles used with the food items the same in both places?
3. Think about reasons for any differences you might see.

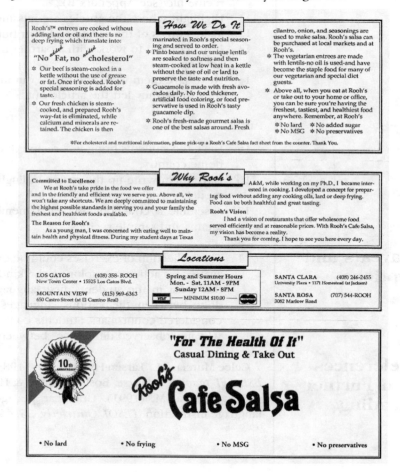

Appetizers

SOUPS & SALADS

All of our soups are made from scratch.

	Cup	Bowl
Chicken Soup	$1.25	$1.95
Mixed Bean Soup	$1.25	$1.95
Chili Bean (Veg.)	$1.25	$1.95
Dinner Salad	$1.25	$1.95

NACHOS $2.95
Crisp pile of Rooh's® Toastilla™ chips covered with frijoles and cheese. Garnished with sour cream and served with fresh salsa.

CHEESE QUESSADILLA ... $3.95

FINGER BURRITOS

Flour tortillas filled with frijoles and cheddar cheese. Served with fresh salsa

3 in a basket $2.95
5 in a basket $4.95

GUACAMOLE

DIPS & CHIPS $2.95
Four ounces of Freshly made guacamole served with plenty of Rooh's toastilla chips and garnished with pico de gallo. (We only use fresh avocado.)

Kid-a-Rooh™
$2.95

For children under 10. All meals are served with 6 oz. soft drink. Your choice of chicken, beef or vegetarian.

QUESADILLA

FINGER BURRITOS (2)

SOFT TACO (1)

Sides & Extras

Chips & Salsa, 4 oz.	$1.75
Guacamole, 2 oz.	95¢
Sour Cream or Cheese, 2 oz.	95¢
Beans, or Lentils or Rice (cup)	$1.25
Rice & Bean (dish)	$1.95
Two flour or corn tortillas with butter	95¢
Pico de gallo or Salsa, 2 oz.	50¢
One Soft Taco	$2.95

Desserts

Flan	$1.99

Flans are made fresh by Rooh's gourmet foods; they contain milk, eggs and are low in sugar.

Copyright © May 1994

Entrees

1: All Entrees are served with a basket of chips and salsa in-house.
2: You can choose pinto beans, chili beans or Rooh's favorite, lentil beans in any of the entrees.
3: You may choose corn tortilla in some of the entrees. Please ask server.
4: Entrees with * are served with a cup of soup, salad, rice or beans of your choice.

TACO SALAD $5.95
A large salad made with plenty of fresh mixed lettuce, sliced tomatoes and Rooh's Toastilla™ chips. Garnished with cheese and olives.
Shredded Chicken
Lean Ground Beef
Vegetarian (Lentil, Frijoles, Chili or Combo)

TOSTADA $5.95
A layer of Rooh's Toastilla™ chips, beans and your choice of topping. Covered with fresh green lettuce,garnished with cheese and pico de gallo.
Shredded Chicken
Lean Ground Beef
Vegetarian - Lentil

* PAELLA DE ROOH'S™ $6.95
A Rooh's creation. A complete meal, rice, beans, cheese, tomatoes and olives and topping of your choice. Garnished with pico de gallo.
Shredded Chicken
Lean Ground Beef
Vegetarian (Lentil or Chili)

PAPAROSA™ $6.95
Slice baked potato with beans, cheese, diced tomatoes, olives and topping of your choice.
Shredded Chicken
Lean Ground Beef
Vegetarian (Chili or Lentil)

BURRITO $5.95
A large flour tortillas filled with tasty beans & rice and choice of filling. Garnished with sour cream, pico de gallo, and cheese.
Shredded Chicken
Lean Ground Beef
Vegetarian (Bean, Chili or Lentil) ....

NACHOS $5.95
A layer of Rooh's Toastilla™ chips covered with frijoles & Cheese. Garnished with sour cream, guacamole and pico de gallo.
Vegetarian (Bean & Cheese)
Shredded Chicken
Lean Ground Beef

* FAJITA KABAB™ $7.95
Another Rooh's creation. Twin skewers of grilled chicken or beef and one skewer of freshly grilled vegetables with three steamed corn or flour tortillas. Garnished with pico de gallo and sour cream.
Steak, Chicken, or Combo Fajita

* ENCHILADA DE ROOH'S .. $6.95
Your choice of two corn or flour tortillas served vegetarian or with meat. Enchiladas are topped with Rooh's enchilada sauce. Garnished with pico de gallo and served with rice.
Shredded Chicken
Lean Ground Beef
Vegetarian - Lentil, Cheese

* ROLITOS™ $6.95
A Rooh's creation. Two flour tortillas filled with meat and a third filled with beans. Rolled, baked, and garnished with cheese, pico de gallo guacamole and sour cream.
Shredded Chicken, Lean Ground Beef, Vegetarian (Lentil), Combo

SOFT TACOS

Your choice of shredded chicken, lean ground beef, or vegetarian (guacamole, frijoles, or lentils).

Basket of any 2 combination	$4.95
Basket of any 3 combination	$6.95

* PANCAKE PIZZA™ $6.95
One more of Rooh's creations. Three layers of flour tortillas with cheddar cheese and your choice of filling. Garnished with Monterey jack cheese, olives and diced tomatoes.
Shredded Chicken, Lean Ground Beef
Vegetarian (Lentil)

* QUESADILLA $5.95
A large flour tortilla filled with cheddar & Monterey jack cheese, frijoles and your choice of filling. Grilled and garnished with sour cream and pico de gallo.
Shredded Chicken
Lean Ground Beef
Vegetarian (Frijoles or Lentils)

Daily Specials

Lunch $4.95
with a drink.

Dinner $6.95
with soup or salad.
Ask Server Please

Beverages

Beer - Imported	$2.75
- Domestic	$2.25
Wine, Sangaria, Marga Rooha™	$2.95
Soft drinks, Tea, Coffee	95¢
Natural juices & mineral waters	$1.25
Milk	75¢

Appendix B: Sample Recipes

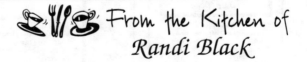 From the Kitchen of
Randi Black

Belva Black's Barbecue Chicken (North Carolina)

⅓ cup water
⅓ cup oil or butter
⅓ cup vinegar
juice of 1 lemon
red pepper and garlic salt
1 chicken

Soak chicken in mixture overnight. Cover with foil. Bake 1 hour at 400 degrees. Uncover and brown on broil.

Used with permission of Randi Black.

From the Kitchen of
Randi Black

May Miner's Apple Dessert

⅔ cup sugar
1 beaten egg
3 T flour
1½ tsp. baking powder
⅛ tsp. salt
1 tsp. vanilla
⅓ cup nuts
1 cup chopped apples

Cream first five ingredients. Grease pan. Add mixture. Bake at 350° for 30 minutes. Cut in squares. Serve with ice cream.

Used with permission of Randi Black.

Contributor

Randi Freeman teaches at Central Washington University, in the United States.

Tomatoes, Etc.

Levels
Intermediate +

Aims
Review, practice, and
learn new food and
spice vocabulary

Class Time
30 minutes

Preparation Time
5 minutes before
first class
20–30 minutes before
second class

Resources
Large tomato
Jar or can of a product
containing tomatoes as
an ingredient (e.g.,
ketchup, chili, or salsa)

This activity gives students an opportunity to pool their knowledge of certain vocabulary, as well as a context that motivates them to find out the words they do not already know.

Procedure

1. Put the tomato and the jar or can on the teacher's desk so that everyone can see. Ask the class to name each of the items, and then ask them to describe the relationship between the two (i.e., one is an ingredient of the other).
2. Brainstorm with the class as many other food items that contain tomatoes as you can, and write the ideas on the chalkboard (e.g., tomato soup, minestrone, pizza, spaghetti sauce, salsa, V-8 juice, tomato juice). Try to have at least one third as many items as there are students in the class.
3. Go back to the jar or can on the desk and ask the class to try to name the other ingredients, besides tomatoes, that are in the product. Write their ideas on the board and help them with words they may not know. Check their answers with the label on the jar or can (skipping the chemical ingredients) and inform them of the actual ingredients.
4. Put students into groups of three and ask each group to choose one of the foods (containing tomatoes) listed on the chalkboard. As each group chooses an item, put a check next to it to indicate that it has been taken and may not be chosen by any other group.
5. Inform the groups that they must now try to figure out all the ingredients—other than tomatoes—of their chosen food item. Walk around the class helping with vocabulary as needed. Once they have completed their lists, they should write them on the board and submit a copy to the teacher.

6. Go over the lists on the chalkboard, discussing the appropriateness of the choices and pointing out similarities and differences among the ingredients found alongside tomatoes.

7. Tell each group that by the next class, someone in each group must bring a jar, can, box, or other container of the food they were working on to verify the ingredients (or look in a supermarket and copy the ingredients). If it is not a packaged item, then someone in the group must bring in the recipe, with ingredients translated into English if necessary.

8. In the next class, compare the student lists of ingredients with the actual ingredients as written on the product labels. In case students forget to bring in their food items, it is a good idea to have a back-up list of ingredients copied from actual labels at home or in the supermarket (see Appendix).

Caveats and Options

1. Other foods besides tomatoes can also be used, such as potatoes, corn, beans, milk, and so on.

2. This activity can lead to discussion of students' native foods, which they may want to describe for the rest of the class using the new ingredient vocabulary that they have been learning.

3. It is helpful to have some visual support for certain typical ingredient items, such as garlic, parsley, basil, oregano, and other herbs and spices, either in the form of pictures or realia.

**Appendix:
Sample
Labels**

Reprinted with permission from The Salsa Factory.

Contributor

Victoria Holder, ESL instructor at San Francisco State University and San Francisco City College, in the United States, has recently published a teacher's resource book on practicing grammar without paper.

Also available from TESOL

The Handbook of Funding Opportunities in the Field of TESOL
Stephen Stoynoff and Terry Camacho

More Than a Native Speaker:
An Introduction for Volunteers Teaching Abroad
Don Snow

New Ways in Content-Based Instruction
Donna M. Brinton and Peter Master, Editors

New Ways in English for Specific Purposes
Peter Master and Donna M. Brinton, Editors

New Ways in Teaching Adults
Marilyn Lewis, Editor

New Ways in Teaching Culture
Alvino E. Fantini, Editor

New Ways in Teaching English at the Secondary Level
Deborah J. Short

New Ways in Teaching Young Children
Linda Schinke-Llano and Rebecca Rauff, Editors

New Ways in Using Communicative Games in Language Teaching
Nikhat Shameem and Makhan Tickoo, Editors

New Ways of Classroom Assessment
James Dean Brown, Editor

New Ways of Using Drama and Literature in Language Teaching
Valerie Whiteson, Editor

New Ways of Using Computers in Language Teaching
Tim Boswood, Editor

Reading and Writing in More Than One Language:
Lessons for Teachers
Elizabeth Franklin, Editor

Tasks for Independent Language Learning
David Gardner and Lindsay Miller, Editors

Teaching in Action: Case Studies From Second Language Classrooms
Jack C. Richards, Editor

For more information, contact
Teachers of English to Speakers of Other Languages, Inc.
700 South Washington Street, Suite 200
Alexandria, Virginia 22314 USA
Tel 703-836-0774 • Fax 703-836-7864 • publ@tesol.edu •
http://www.tesol.edu/

Founded 1966